Additional Praise for *Let's Close a Deal*

"Christine Clifford has obviously studied the art of the deal—her approach to deal-making is the 'real deal'!"

—**Monty Hall, host of television's *"Let's Make a Deal"*®**

"Just because you have a brilliant idea, valuable venture, or beneficial product/service—doesn't mean it will succeed. You must be able to close the deal and get a 'yes' from customers and decision makers. This intriguing, useful book shows how."

—**Sam Horn, Author of *POP!* and *THE EYEBROW TEST***

"Let's Close a Deal is a treasure trove of practical ideas to help you create brand-new sales and delight clients with surprisingly little effort. I love Christine Clifford's triple-win approach to selling."

—**Graham McGregor, President of TWOMAC Consulting, Ltd;**
Creator of *The Unfair Business Advantage Report*

"Christine Clifford has demystified the concept of deal making, while providing a step-by-step framework that any aspiring entrepreneur, regardless of their product or service, can use to take their business to a whole new level. *Let's Close a Deal* not only contains a host of very smart and practical information, it is also highly inspirational. This is a great book."

—**Andrew Griffiths, Australia's #1 Small Business Author**

"At a time when 'business ethics' seems to have become an oxymoron, Christine Clifford shares valuable insights on how salespeople can be successful and also principled. As she puts it in elegantly simple terms, 'It is never okay to close a deal that is only self-serving.' I highly recommend this book."

—**Chris Lowney, author of *Heroic Leadership:***
Best Practices from a 450-Year Old Company
That Changed the World* and *Heroic Living: Discover
Your Purpose and Change the World

"I started reading *Let's Close a Deal* because I read everything that Christine Clifford writes, but I finished reading it because everything she says is so on-target for my own business and for the organizations we work with. This is much more than a book about closing deals—it's a handbook of priceless advice for building relationships and building a successful business. Anyone who is in sales—and that's all of us in one way or another—can benefit from the wisdom, insights, and humor that Christine weaves into this wonderful book."

—Joe Tye, CEO of Values Coach Inc.
and author of *All Hands on Deck:*
8 Essential Lessons for Building
a Culture of Ownership

"Christine Clifford proves that selling is never about closing. It's always something we forgot or neglected to do earlier in the sales process. She peppers her narrative with engaging and 'wow' stories. Build relationships, don't take 'no' for an answer, engage your creativity, and ask for referrals—powerful reminders for all salespeople."

—Joanne S. Black, author of
No More Cold Calling™

"What a fantastic job Christine Clifford has done with *Let's Close a Deal* It is an incredibly inspiring read and jam-packed full of easy-to-understand, practical information which anyone can implement to enjoy increased sales, increased profits and increased fun. *Let's Close a Deal* is an absolute must-have!"

—Paul Vujnovich, entrepreneur
and founder of FindMyRealEstateAgent.co.nz

LET'S CLOSE A DEAL

**Turn Contacts into Paying Customers for
Your Company, Product, Service or Cause**

CHRISTINE CLIFFORD

WILEY

Cover image: © Andrea Leone/iStockphoto
Cover design: Jeff Faust

Copyright © Christine Clifford 2013. All rights reserved.
Published by John Wiley & Sons, Inc., Hoboken, New Jersey.

Published simultaneously in Canada.

No part of this publication may be reproduced, stored in a retrieval system, or transmitted in any form or
by any means, electronic, mechanical, photocopying, recording, scanning, or otherwise, except as
permitted under Section 107 or 108 of the 1976 United States Copyright Act, without either the prior
written permission of the Publisher, or authorization through payment of the appropriate per-copy fee to
the Copyright Clearance Center, 222 Rosewood Drive, Danvers, MA 01923, (978) 750-8400, fax (978)
646-8600, or on the web at www.copyright.com. Requests to the Publisher for permission should be
addressed to the Permissions Department, John Wiley & Sons, Inc., 111 River Street, Hoboken, NJ
07030, (201) 748-6011, fax (201) 748-6008, or online at www.wiley.com/go/permissions.

Limit of Liability/Disclaimer of Warranty: While the publisher and author have used their best efforts in
preparing this book, they make no representations or warranties with respect to the accuracy or
completeness of the contents of this book and specifically disclaim any implied warranties of
merchantability or fitness for a particular purpose. No warranty may be created or extended by sales
representatives or written sales materials. The advice and strategies contained herein may not be suitable for
your situation. You should consult with a professional where appropriate. Neither the publisher nor the
author shall be liable for damages arising herefrom.

For general information about our other products and services, please contact our Customer Care
Department within the United States at (800) 762-2974, outside the United States at (317) 572-3993, or
fax (317) 572-4002.

Wiley publishes in a variety of print and electronic formats and by print-on-demand. Some material
included with standard print versions of this book may not be included in e-books or in print-on-demand.
If this book refers to media such as a CD or DVD that is not included in the version you purchased, you
may download this material at http://booksupport.wiley.com. For more information about Wiley
products, visit www.wiley.com.

Library of Congress Cataloging-in-Publication Data:
Clifford, Christine.
   Let's close a deal : turn contacts into paying customers for your company, product, service or cause /
Christine Clifford.
pages cm
   ISBN 978-1-118-52155-7 (cloth); ISBN 978-1-118-59675-3 (ebk); ISBN 978-1-118-59677-7 (ebk);
ISBN 978-1-118-59692-0 (ebk)
  1. Selling. 2. Customer relations. I. Title.
   HF5438.25.C55 2013
   658.85–dc23
                                                                        2012049237

Printed in the United States of America
10 9 8 7 6 5 4 3 2 1

*In memory of Jack Lindstrom,
a partner extraordinaire with whom
I closed one of the biggest deals of my life:
his friendship.*

Contents

Contents

Foreword

*Y*ou're wrong . . . if you think this book is about how to peddle products and services and pressure people to buy what they don't want or need, or if you think this is a book full of psychobabble about human behavior in buying or selling.

Instead, Christine Clifford has methodically addressed the subject of sales and selling in an illuminating, articulate, sincere, and provocative manner. I can tell you from personal experience that it is impossible to say "no" to her. And in her writing, she draws on her well-developed sales skills and important lessons she has learned about selling in a passionate way that will allow you to apply and benefit from her advice immediately.

Christine is a survivor . . . of breast cancer, of divorce, of domestic violence, of financial difficulty, of having to make it in a world that isn't always kind to those who are successful, especially a woman. She has worked her way through each challenge by applying the skills that she learned and developed in sales. She understands the difference between high-pressure selling to get someone to buy versus solving that person's problem or meeting his or her need with a well-conceived solution.

Having served as chairman and a member of the boards of directors for many companies and as a president and CEO of large successful enterprises, I have observed the good, the bad, and the ugly salespeople and processes. Unfortunately, the good salespeople and processes are the exception, not the rule.

As a junior executive early in my career, my mentor—several years my senior—took me to lunch one day and, with his cigar smoked down to the last inch and pinched tightly between his teeth, said, "Sheffert, do you know what the difference is between the successful people in life and the unsuccessful people?"

I quickly told him that I suspected it was their willingness to work hard, to which he said in a kind of agitated response, "No, that's part of it, but that's not it . . . so guess again." I then offered that perhaps it was that they worked smarter than the others. Once again he bit down on his cigar a little tighter and said, "No, no, that's important, but that's not it either!" Seeing that he was becoming impatient with my surface responses, I suggested he just tell me the reason.

He took off his glasses, moved his cigar over to the side of his mouth, and stared directly into my eyes. "Successful people do not do one, or just a few, but a whole bunch of little things that unsuccessful people aren't willing to do." He went on to give me examples of what he meant.

He told me to remember this because, although it may not seem profound then, I would see the wisdom in it later in my career. Well, he was spot on, and as I read Christine's manuscript for this book, I realized that she was sharing with her readers the many little things that my mentor shared with me—things that separate the successful from the unsuccessful salespeople in this world.

This book is not intended for those who think they have all the answers about selling; rather, it's intended for those who are interested in selling more and bettering themselves. If you are already a successful salesperson, then you will enjoy this read and still get value from it. If you are not selling as much as you would like, then you *must* read this book because you will be profoundly affected by it.

—Mark W. Sheffert

* * *

Mr. Sheffert is the chairman and CEO of Manchester Companies, Inc., a Minneapolis-based financial and management advisory firm. He is a nationally recognized leader who has served on more than 45 boards of directors and was chairman of half, including some of the nation's largest financial institutions, health care, and airline organizations. Prior to founding Manchester, he was president of the eighth-largest bank holding company in the United States and also served as chairman and CEO of one of the top five trust companies in the nation. Mr. Sheffert is a prolific author who has written more than 250 articles and currently writes a monthly column for three business publications.

Acknowledgments

I thank my parents, who have both been gone for an incredibly long time, for teaching me resiliency and manners as a child. Thanks for letting me play dress up as a young girl and for allowing me to play the role of chief executive officer (CEO) when all the other girls wanted to play princess. Thanks for never squashing my dreams.

I thank my two sons, Tim Clifford and Brooks Clifford, and their significant others, Chris Hiedeman and Oksana Sukhovirska, for being the loves of my life. You bring me joy and laughter daily. Skylar, you, too.

My brothers, Greg and James Meyer, and my beloved sister, Pam, and her husband, Nick Haros, are in my heart and on my mind daily. I love how we are all so close, even though far away. Thanks for always being here for me.

To my extended family: Stephanie Meyer, Kristin and JT Thompson, the boys (Ryken, Kian, and Sorin), Bette, John, and Bill Clifford, thank you for being there for me and my boys as I forged my career and battled cancer. I am forever in your debt.

To Matt Holt, my publisher; Adrianna Johnson, my editor; and Deborah Schindlar and all the folks at John Wiley & Sons, thanks for helping me close this deal.

A special thanks to Bob Brown and Bill Bartels, who taught me everything I needed to know to close a deal in my years at SPAR Marketing Services. We had it all going on, and it was an amazing—and fun—journey. Thanks for believing in me.

I couldn't begin to thank all my friends, but I'll try: Dr. Dan Ahlberg, Mary McNutt, Jean Golden, Steve Schussler and Sunhi Ryan, Jeff Hiedeman, Brian Gierhan, Dawn and Jon Earl, Liz and Jim Robertson, Margie and Mark

Sborov, Dr. Burt Schwartz, the Full Moon gals (Lauren Shapiro, Mary Harlow, Amy Silverman, Parrel Caplan, Wendy Cammins, Susan Jacobs, Susan Brun, Janet Coleman, Geri Rosenberg, and Lynne Assardo), Mary Ann Heine, Bob and Virginia Carlson, Kathy and Pat Lewis, Aija and Tom Meehan, Cheryl Sandeen, Pat and Bucky Zimmerman, Jaime Hansen, Jan and Jack Moore, Adele Brellenthin, the Divas (Amber Serwat, Linda Margl, Deborah Gibson, Joelle Pink, Susan Gran, Susan Garfield, Michelle Palmer, Bonnie Bakken, and all of our volunteers), Alison Nelson, Barb Demos, Barb Greenberg, Barb Rosen, Jackie Lindstrom, Bev and Bruce Nickerson, Joe Regan, CJ Dubé, Dawn Stebbing, the "Gianni's Girls" (Diane Miller, Laura Osman, Carolyn Friedberg, Ginny Wallack, Terri Huml), Eddie Leigh, Gail Tilsner, Gregg Eggington, Susan Allender, Gerald McCullagh, Gregory Brassil, Jim Greer, Tom Schmidt, Isaac Diaz, Jeff Lillemoe, Jeff Evans, Jill Peterson, Paula Bergs, Stephanie Hofkenke, Karin Preus, Keri Pickett, Kim Valentini, Mary Schmid, Shan White, Mindy Montano, Sue Bleecker, Nancy Van Dyken, Rick Swanson, Terry Barth, Tracy Stewart, Neda Weldele, Vicky Rackner, Chuck and Norma Smith, Tracy Stewart, Jennifer Shirley, Carol Ann Usefara, Ryan and Brady Ahlberg, Kate McKenzie, Arnold Palmer, Dr. Buck Brown, Annie Brown, Amy Grant, Robert Grant, Sharon Krumme, Larry Gatlin, and Harvey MacKay.

For those of you who haven't been mentioned, it's only because I'm getting old and I'm under deadline. I apologize. My deepest gratitude to all of my clients, sponsors, and vendors of our conferences and to anyone else with whom I've closed a deal. I hope you've enjoyed the ride as much as I have. *Thank you!*

Overview and Introduction

If opportunity doesn't knock, build a door.

—Milton Berle

I n 1975 I sat across from a district manager for Nestlé interviewing for my
first job in sales. A friend from college had recommended me, and he was
already working in a similar position for the company.

Forced to drop out of college during my junior year because my mother
had died from breast cancer and my father, a physician, had undergone
quadruple bypass surgery, my only relevant job experience had been as a senior
secretary for several stockbrokers at a regional firm. After an extensive interview, the district manager thanked me for applying for the position and said,
"I'm sorry, but I can't offer you the job. You have a lot of the qualifications
we're looking for, and you come highly recommended. However, you have no
sales experience."

Arguing, I explained that I would work hard, and couldn't he please just
give me a chance? I could see that the more I begged the more certain he'd
become that he'd made the right decision. As I walked out of the building,
feeling totally dejected, I realized I had gone about the process completely
wrong. I hadn't been able to close the deal because I hadn't positioned myself
properly.

I was so busy thinking about *me* and what that job would do for my
dwindling bank account that I never really talked about what I could do for
him or, better yet, what I could do for his company. I resolved then and there
that I would do what it took to get the necessary sales experience, and I would

learn to position myself in such a way that potential employers would think, "I *have* to hire her. She's just what we're looking for."

We're All Salespeople

When you think about it, our entire lives revolve around selling. It makes no difference if your job title is Project Manager, Director of Client Services, Intern, Executive Administrative Assistant, or Vice President of Marketing. We are all making impressions and representing our company, product, service, or cause with every business-related conversation and interaction.

Whether we sell as part of our business, serve on a committee of a nonprofit organization, negotiate for a new job/car/house, or influence where we have dinner on Friday night, we are pitching, hearing, and closing deals every day. We make our decisions based on the manner in which information is presented to us and what we believe will be the best deal. That is the focus of this book—how to present information so persuasively it increases the likelihood of getting a "yes."

So the question is not, "Am I a salesperson? I thought I was a _____ _____ [fill in the blank: Human Resources Coordinator, Patient Advocate, Virtual Assistant, Architect, Loan Officer, Office Manager . . .]." The *real* question is, "How can I be more effective?"

Goodwill is the one and only asset that competition cannot undersell or destroy.

—Marshall Field

The sales process is not about coercion; it's about compassion. A primary purpose of *Let's Close a Deal* is to introduce the concept that the closing part of a negotiation or sale should honor the people involved instead of taking advantage of them. My goal is to articulate the intuitive process that identifies how and why a deal will appeal to others and then demonstrate in step-by-step detail how to present your deal in such a compelling way that it becomes a fait accompli.

Let's Close a Deal isn't just about the close. It's about the dozens of details that go into the process of the pitch, from establishing Niche Notoriety and building top-of-mind awareness with your target audience to Perk-O-Lating a deal by identifying the surprise bonuses that make or break its success.

Philosophies will be turned upside down as this book encourages you to look for business in all the wrong places so you leave no "store" unturned. You'll learn how to turn a "no" into a "yes" with the three Rs (retreat, reevaluate, and reapproach) and how to thank your customers in spectacular ways so that they'll keep coming back for more.

How will these techniques help you make more money? By enabling you to get along better with your clients and customers, speeding up the time frame of your deals, and making the entire process of selling go more smoothly.

Perhaps most important, this book shows how to make every interaction enjoyable so people *like* doing business with you and *you* like doing business.

As you'll discover, closing a deal isn't just about satisfying your own goals, quotas, and ambitions; it is more a philosophy of life that will lead you to new levels of sales success and satisfaction. It will put the fun back into your work, volunteerism, and relationships and give you new insight into how you can prospect ethically everywhere you go. You'll learn how to turn contacts into connections and connections into customers who are loyals for life.

> *One of the finest things you can be is a good example.*
>
> —Jeannie Esposito

Are you wondering what credentials I bring to this book? Are you thinking that you've read many books on how to sell, and you're wondering what I could possible say that hasn't been said before?

Good questions. See, you want additional information before you're convinced it's going to be worth your valuable time to read this book. Here's a little more information about my background that might help close this deal.

Following that discouraging interview in which I was turned down for my first job in sales, I set out on what has become a thoroughly satisfying 30+ year journey into the world of deal making. I got my initiation the hard way, by becoming a route sales driver for Hanes DSD. Do you remember those old L'eggs panty hose vans . . . about the size of a UPS truck? I got to where I could parallel park that baby in downtown Minneapolis during rush hour using only one hand.

In the early 1980s, I was in the right place at the right time and joined SPAR Marketing Services, an international merchandising firm in New York. During my tenure there, I rose to the rank of senior executive vice president and demonstrated the art of closing the deal by signing the largest contract in the history of the retail services industry—an $18-million dollar contract with Procter & Gamble that doubled the size of our company overnight.

In 1994 I was diagnosed with breast cancer. During my treatment and recovery, I discovered there was a need for humorous and helpful products for people with cancer. I wrote my first book, *Not Now . . . I'm Having a No Hair Day!* and created a company called The Cancer Club, which became the largest business of its kind serving the needs of people dealing with cancer. Since starting that organization from scratch, I've had many opportunities to be resourceful in figuring out how to approach decision makers with offers that would interest them in buying our products, sponsoring our fund-raising efforts, and supporting our service-related activities.

I took an enormous risk after my diagnosis of cancer and left my "real" job with salary, benefits, bonuses, and commissions for no "real job" at all: only a dream I had of becoming an author and business owner. Writing my first book launched a career as a professional speaker, and I earned my Certified Speaking Professional (CSP) designation from the National Speakers Association. Fewer than 650 people hold the CSP, putting me in the top 10 percent of professional speakers worldwide. I went on to write six additional books, including coauthoring *You, Inc. The Art of Selling Yourself,* and to provide consulting services to companies and individuals worldwide on sales and marketing strategies.

Hard work, good fortune, fortuitous timing, enduring friendships, much-welcomed laughter, and high expectations have led me to being a top sales producer year after year in a variety of industries. First-person stories from my experiences plus anecdotes from clients and associates are featured throughout this book so that you might learn from our examples. Mark Twain said, "We should learn from the mistakes of others. We don't have time to make them all ourselves." It is my sincerest hope that you learn from my mistakes and accomplishments so you can expedite your own personal and professional successes.

Whether you are new to sales or a seasoned veteran, *Let's Close a Deal* is designed to provide you with a multitude of techniques that can help you close more deals on and off the job. May you embrace and hone these principles, take them to the streets, and become a sales professional par excellence. After all, every day is a great day to close a deal.

Section I

What's the Big Deal?

As long as you're going to be thinking anyway—think BIG!

—Donald Trump

Chapter 1

Let's Define the Deal

Quick. What's the first image that comes to mind when you hear the word *salesperson?* Pushy? Manipulative? Devious? Annoying? Obnoxious? Dishonest? Desperate?

It doesn't have to be that way. Think back to the last time you tried to make a sale. Was your customer excited to take your call, or did he not even bother to return it? Did she compliment your style and approach, or did she tell you to call back in six months?

That's because most of us are focused on selling the wrong thing. We focus on only one aspect of the sale: You pay me this for that, or you give me this for that. We tend to view selling as a "win-win." What's in it for you, and what's in it for me? This book will teach you to focus on "What's in it for three?" There is always a third-party beneficiary of every sale: You, me, and your company, your charity, the people you serve, or your organization stand to benefit from your success. I like to call this the "win-win-win." And if you can always ask yourself the question, "How *many* can benefit from this sale?" instead of "How can *I* benefit from this sale?" then you are well on your way toward closing more deals.

The headlines in the paper blare: "The Architect of the Deal" (as two large insurance companies merge); "It's All About the Deal" (as shoppers line up before dawn to grab the biggest bargains, newest iPhone, or tickets to a once-in-a-lifetime concert); "No Done Deal on Medicare" (as questions are raised about a tentative deal to revamp Medicare); or "Deal Makes Workers Wary" (as employees worried about their jobs watch anxiously as their company is about to be sold). Big deals—and little deals—are happening all around us every minute of every day.

The premise of this book is that you're representing a valuable product, creating a unique service, or passionately championing a cause. Now what? How do you get the world to sit up and pay attention to what you have to offer? Sure, you can sell your product, service, or cause to your friends and family or the local Chamber of Commerce; however, the real money is in positioning yourself to close the deal with major corporations, organizations, charities, or individuals who can propel your business to the next level and beyond.

The first question to ask yourself is: Why would anyone *want* to buy my product or service or participate in my cause? If you yourself can't understand the appeal about what it is you're pitching or selling, how can you expect others to understand? Understanding the motivations of the people you're selling to can greatly increase your opportunity for success. Do your very best to get into their head before you pitch anything. Let me help you get into that head. People will buy from you for 12 basic reasons:

1. They need to replace something that is old, broken, outdated, or inconvenient. They may or may not have a sense of urgency about their purchase.

2. The product or service you have to offer solves a problem. Learn to solve the problem, and you can sell it to the world.

3. Your product or service fills a need or a void.

4. The prospects are risk takers and see potential growth for their future. Stockbrokers, venture capitalists, and entrepreneurs fit in this category.

5. The prospects have outgrown their existing product due to growth, expansion, or technology.

6. The product would be given as a gift and would give others pleasure from receiving it.

7. The prospect wants to be part of the "in crowd" and have what everybody else has.

8. The product or service has a perceived value of equal or greater importance to its worth.

9. The prospect has an obsession about or a collection of the product. They think, "I have to have that."

10. They are being forced to purchase it, perhaps because they broke a law or are mandated to participate.

11. Your competition has dropped the ball. Someone's going to pick it up, so why not you?

12. Because they can. For these people, money is *not* an object.

Before you even begin to position, prepare, and pitch, ask yourself which of these categories you are trying to access. Misreading or miscalculating *need* in the beginning can sabotage your success from the get-go.

So what is the first step toward closing the deal?

Let me tell you the secret that has led me to my goal. My strength lies solely in my tenacity.

—Louis Pasteur (1822–1895)

Turn Your Close Inside Out

Step 1: Prepare People to Expect Your Sales Proposal or Request

Never send something unsolicited, unexpected, or without preconceived value to the buyer.

I was putting the finishing touches on my third cancer book when it occurred to me, "Wouldn't it be cool to get Arnold Palmer to write the Foreword?"

Why Arnold Palmer? Well, in addition to being a household name, he's a cancer survivor, as are other members of his family. And he is a longtime friend.

First, I contacted Arnie's office and spoke to his secretary. "I am working on a new book titled *Cancer Has Its Privileges: Stories of Hope and Laughter* and would like to ask Arnie to write the Foreword. Is this something you think he'd consider and be interested in?" I knew it would be fairly easy for her to grant my request. After all, this book dealt with a subject important to him. She suggested I put my request in writing.

So I wrote a letter to Arnie asking if he'd write the Foreword and sent it off with a just-finished copy of the manuscript. I even highlighted and bookmarked a story in the book about golf, so he'd read it first. Within three weeks, I got back a handwritten letter from the "King" himself.

Dear Christine:

You know how much I care about you. You know I think the work you are doing on behalf of cancer patients is spectacular. But the truth [of] the matter is that I am far too busy to be able to sit down and write a Foreword that could possibly do justice to your work. More importantly, I have never, ever put my name on a product or an endorsement that isn't either a product of Arnold Palmer Industries, or the product of one of my corporate sponsors.

I guess most people would call that a "no."

However, I didn't become a successful salesperson by taking the first "no" as the final "no."

So, instead of giving up, I contacted Dr. Clarence H. Brown III. "Dr. Buck," as he's affectionately known, was the chief executive officer (CEO) of the MD Anderson Cancer Center Orlando, and I'd had the opportunity to work with him on numerous projects. I had always done my best to exceed his expectations (one of the important components for closing a deal). Over the years, I had donated books to his library, participated in his annual fundraiser, and delivered a pro bono presentation as a way of showing my appreciation for his scheduling me for several other paid speaking engagements. As a way of thanking him for his business in a way that was memorable and life-lasting (a key component to creating loyals for life;

see Chapter 14), I had arranged for Buck and his wife Annie to receive complimentary tickets to an annual golf tournament I hosted to raise money for breast cancer research in Minneapolis.

As a result of this above-and-beyond service, when I asked Dr. Buck to write the Foreword to my book, he not only accepted on the spot, he was so honored to be included in the project that he asked, "Is there anything else I can do to help you with *our* book?"

Did I mention that Buck is Arnold's personal oncologist and that Arnie donated a wing to the MD Anderson Cancer Center Orlando?

I told Buck what had happened with Arnold, and Buck continued to help me brainstorm options. "Since time is a concern to Arnie," he pointed out, "why don't we ask him to write the Introduction? It's only a paragraph or two so it's a far simpler process. You and I can draft it, and then I will drive it over to his house and sit on his couch until he signs off on it! Won't we three make a fabulous team?"

Great idea, and that's exactly what we did. Buck and I wrote it, he drove it over, and Arnie signed it! As a result of reworking that deal so it had more appeal, Arnold Palmer agreed to give his first-ever book endorsement to *Cancer Has Its Privileges*.

But more important is this: I didn't just mail off a request to Arnie to write the Foreword or Introduction. I first called his office and then with permission sent my inquiry. I once heard that Oprah Winfrey at the height of her original television show was receiving more than 10,000 unsolicited products/books/gadgets and anything else that could be put in a box *weekly* in her offices. Did any of these get looked at? Rarely. They ended up going in a storage room where employees could sort through them and take them home for their own families or friends. At the end of the year, whatever wasn't taken was donated to charity.

Don't end up in a storage room. Prepare your prospect to receive what it is you have to offer. How do you do that? By calling, e-mailing, texting, or dropping by someone's office face-to-face. A useful strategy would be, "Bill, my name is Christine Clifford and I understand that you are the person responsible for purchasing office incentives for your employees and clients. My company DigiClean has just created an ultrafine microfiber screen cleaner that sticks to your mobile phone or case. Clients can customize these quarter-sized cleaners with their company logo or contact information. May I send you a few product samples?"

By opening the door to accepting a sales proposition, you have increased your chances of having your prospect say, "Yes. Please do."

Step 2: Prepare Yourself to Retreat, Reevaluate, and Reapproach Your Contact

Why do I share the story of Arnold? Because it shows that if we *don't* close a deal, it's often because we gave up at the first "no." I've learned that with innovative brainstorming, gentle persistence, and the three Rs—retreat, reevaluate, and reapproach—we can often turn an initial "no" into an eventual "yes," all the while creating a win-win-win relationship that benefits everyone involved. Ready to find out how to do that? Read on.

Sometimes we have to turn our closing inside out so that we can look at it in a totally different way. When people reject our request, it's often because we didn't make our offer sufficiently compelling (what's in it for me?), we ignored their needs, or we simply failed to clearly define the value or long- and short-term benefits of what we are selling.

Certainly, I knew what was in it for *me* by asking for Arnie's endorsement. He'd bring immediate name recognition and added allure to my work. People with cancer would think, "If Arnold Palmer can get through this experience, so can I." Most definitely a win for me.

Let's look at this scenario through Dr. Buck's eyes. He was excited about being included in a book because it was a first-time experience for him. He viewed it as a partnership with himself, Arnold, and me, and it was a way of paying respect to us both as patients and friends. Furthermore, whether this was a conscious decision or not, his association with this project would gain nationwide attention for his work and his cancer center. A win for Dr. Buck.

As for Arnold? I had originally ignored his needs regarding time and loyalty to his sponsors. I hadn't made it clear I was willing to help in any way I could to make this easy. And I had complicated his life even more by asking him to read an entire manuscript. No win here.

After his initial "no," I resorted to an important closing principle: retreat, reevaluate, and reapproach. Without completely ignoring Arnie's initial response, I looked at other options and thought, "Who could I get to write the Foreword whom I admire and who might possibly help get Arnie involved?" By asking Buck to write the Foreword and by asking for his help, I brought in a second mind to brainstorm innovative approaches.

By physically sitting down and talking to Arnie, Dr. Buck was able to relieve Arnie's anxieties about the amount of time and commitment required. Through his own enthusiasm for the project, Buck was able to convince Arnie that it would be a win for him to get involved. Arnie would be doing a great service for cancer patients; he'd be helping his friend Christine, and he'd be partnering with Buck, an important role model for his family. A classic win-win-win.

How can you anticipate ahead of time why your deal might not appeal? Ask yourself:

- Is what I am asking for (time, money, people, resources) reasonable?
- Would what I am offering appeal to me personally? My mother? My next-door neighbor? My current client base?
- Do I have the answers to all the questions that might be asked of me? If not, am I prepared to get the answers within 24 hours?
- Can I deliver what I am promising?

You can get everything in life you want if you will just help enough other people get what they want.

—Zig Ziglar

Let's Define the Deal

The win-win-win factor means that we need to approach sales not just as "What's in it for you and me?" We need to approach sales as "What's in it for *three?*" There is *always* a third-party beneficiary in every sales transaction. By preparing and troubleshooting ahead of time, you can often nip a "no" in the bud. If you package and pitch your deals with that in mind, you can usually turn an initial "no" into a "yes." Here's one of my favorite examples of someone who pitched his deal in a way that made it easy for the customer to say yes.

Sharpen Your Close

My doorbell rang on a Wednesday afternoon a few weeks before the holidays. I answered the bell and an impeccably dressed young man stuck his hand out and greeted me with a smile. "Mrs. Clifford? I'm Tyler Hagemo. I'm sure you know my younger brother, Nate, who is in your son Brooks's class. In fact, I believe they play hockey together. I graduated last year, and I know your other son, Tim." (He created connections; see Chapter 6.)

"Why, yes, Tyler, what can I do for you today?" I inquired.

"Please know I am not trying to sell you anything, but I am involved in a program that gives me credit toward college scholarships if I can make a certain number of presentations per week. I have already given your neighbors, the Borg's and the Lewis's, a presentation, and I was wondering if you would be so kind as to allow me to make a presentation to you as well? If this isn't a convenient time for you, I'd be happy to schedule a time that works better. My product is a beautiful set of knives, and my entire presentation shouldn't take more than 15 minutes." (Step 1: He prepared me to expect his proposal or request.)

I couldn't help but chuckle to myself as I thought, "Why don't I give him a break and help him out?" He'd appealed to my heart and soul since we, too, were saving money for our high school senior to head off to college. I also knew that I didn't need any knives, so I felt safe in listening to Tyler's pitch. After all, if my neighbors had sat through his presentation, surely I could do the same. And it *was* only 15 minutes.

Tyler went right to work, carefully pulling out and displaying a beautiful set of knives. He referred to me quite often by name, "Mrs. Clifford, do you and Mr. Clifford have a knife that can cut like *this*?" He sliced and diced with a speed and accuracy never before seen in the Clifford household.

"How long have you had your current knives, Mrs. Clifford? Why don't you show them to me and let me point out how *our* knives are superior?" (He did a great job of addressing the competition and comparing himself favorably to the other "deals" on the market.)

"Have you bought that 'special something' for Mr. Clifford yet?" he asked.

I thought, "You know, I really haven't gotten him anything *special* . . . " (He targeted my need and desire to buy my husband a gift he'd like and use.)

"How much *are* these knives, Tyler?" I asked, reminding myself that we really didn't *need* them.

"$750.00," came Tyler's reply with total confidence. Before I could scoop my jaw off the floor, Tyler jumped right in. "I know you might be thinking these are expensive knives. They have a lifetime guarantee, however, and we can even set up a payment plan if you'd like."

I said, "Tyler, they *are* beautiful knives, and you've done an excellent presentation. I really can't afford them right now."

Tyler didn't hesitate. He said, "If you purchase these knives today, I'll even throw in this special pair of scissors that cut through *anything*. The scissors alone are a $100 value. Would you like me to demonstrate the scissors?" (Tyler was both Perk-O-Lating the deal [see Chapter 9], and reevaluating and reapproaching the deal by sweetening it.)

After a quick demonstration of the most amazing pair of scissors I had ever seen, Tyler turned to me and simply said, "Can I write up your order now, Mrs. Clifford?"

To my amazement, I ordered three sets: one for my husband, one for my father-in-law, and one for a rainy day. Tyler Hagemo had closed the deal. Why? He didn't take no for an answer, and he continued to present information that made his product appealing. In the end, I thought, "I have to have that" (IHTHT; see Chapter 4)—the sure sign of a winning pitch. Best of all, his was a win-win-win interaction. He got that scholarship to college, my husband and father-in-law liked their gifts, and we're *still* using those knives!

You can't just sell products. You have to sell benefits and solutions.

—Anonymous

Tyler's positioning, preparation, and pitch were brilliant. Let's define exactly what made Tyler's sales presentation pitch perfect.

- From the beginning, Tyler knew who his *targeted market* was: community members who may know him, his brother, or another member of his family. He wasn't going into strange neighborhoods (or stores; see Chapter 5) that knew nothing about him or his product.

- Tyler looked presentable, was nicely dressed, and made a good first impression.

- He had a *mission statement* (see Chapter 2) for himself and his product that was concise, succinct, and compelling.

- Tyler made a *connection* (see Chapter 6) with me by mentioning my kids and my neighbors. He wasn't just "cold calling"; he came with a link that gave me incentive to listen.

- He *prepared* me for the sales pitch by stating that he wasn't selling anything, but I could still help him out just by listening to his pitch.

- He *was flexible and attentive to my needs* by offering to reschedule at a more convenient time, if necessary. He was conscious of *my* needs (time and money) and addressed them right away.

- His *positioning statement* was compelling: He was trying to help fund his college tuition, yet at the same time offer something that might be of interest to me.

- Tyler *wasted no time* getting right to the point and provided clarity, value, and purpose to his product. There was never a doubt in my mind as to what it was he was trying to sell me.

- He was *attentive* during his presentation, constantly pulling me in by using my name and referring to others in my family who might benefit from his product (not just thinking about "you and me," but thinking about three: win-win-win).

- Tyler's presentation demonstrated why his product was:
  - Unique
  - Beneficial
  - Special
  - Cost-effective
  - Necessary

   He also compared his product to the other "big deals" out there in the market place: the *competition*. Clearly, his product left the others in the dust.

- He stated the *cost* of his product with clarity and confidence. He never tried to backpedal or justify his cost. Negotiation wasn't a part of the deal.

- He understood the concept of the three Rs: *retreat, reevaluate,* and *reapproach* (see Chapter 12).

- He gently *overcame my objections* by being compassionate, explaining the lifetime guarantee, and offering a payment plan.

- He wouldn't take *the first "no" as the final "no."*

- He *Perk-O-Lated* the deal by offering the "free" scissors, a $100 value (see Chapter 9).

- Tyler led me to the point of believing "I have to have that" (the IHTHT theory).

13

Let's Define the Deal

- He *asked for the order* (see Chapter 10). Some salespeople are indirect. They wait for prospects to say they're ready to buy instead of stating outright, "Would you like me to write this up now?" Don't forget to ask!

Tyler Hagemo was 19 years old. He was fresh out of high school with "no sales experience," yet he had so successfully strategized the sales process that I was ready to say "yes." If he can sell knives to *me*, then you, too, can position, prepare, and pitch *your* product or service with equal or greater success. Garfield the Cat has always said it best: "Big deal. . . "

What is it that is going to make your deal different from all the rest? The next section explains in detail how you can apply these techniques to your next big sale.

Here's the Real Deal

- There is always a third-party beneficiary of every sale. Create the win-win-win.
- Increase your success by understanding the motivations of the people you're selling to.
- Prepare people to expect your sales proposal or request.
- Retreat, reevaluate, and reapproach if you are turned down.

Let's Prepare the Deal

Life is like an ever-shifting kaleidoscope—a slight change and all patterns alter.

—Sharon Salzberg

Chapter 2

Let's Package a Deal

A lot of times when a package says, "Open Other End," I purposely open the end where it says that.

—George Carlin

It's your birthday. Your three best friends meet you to celebrate and buy you lunch. Gifts are set on the table: One is from Target; one is from Macy's; the third is from Tiffany's.

You're probably already doing it—making a decision about which will be the best gift. Why? Because we're visual and what you are looking at is an important piece of closing a deal. It's called packaging, and like it or not, it plays a crucial role in sales.

Just like a kaleidoscope, the smallest tweak in the way we package our deal can be the difference between success and failure. Have you heard any of the following comments after making your sales pitch? Wrong color, wrong size, too big, too small, too short, too tall, too expensive, too cheap, too soft, too hard, doesn't go with the rest of my things, too fat, too skinny, too much? If so, this chapter will help you anticipate and eliminate those objections so they don't sink your deal.

Close Horse

Marianne Svihlik is a breast cancer survivor who lives with her husband Chuck in the tiny town of Forreston, Illinois. Marianne had turned her passion for the cause of breast cancer into a small business by developing some beautiful ornaments, the Guardian Angel Feather Ornament and the Breast Cancer Ornament.

Over the course of two years, working out of her basement and the garage, Marianne sold about 500 of these handcrafted ornaments to family, friends, coworkers, and customers who found the small website she created. Then Marianne found The Cancer Club website and e-mailed me to ask if we would sell her ornaments along with the other products on our site.

Quickly logging on to her site, I viewed the ornaments from the simple Polaroid photographs she posted. They were beautiful; however, I reluctantly decided we couldn't sell her product because they were made of glass and all I could think about was "damages." The thought of shipping, receiving, packing, and cracking made my head spin. I wrote her back and told her she had done a marvelous job tapping into her creativity, and I admired her for being a survivor like myself and for using her skills to further our cause. But I couldn't carry her product due to its fragile material.

Marianne, however, was not one to take "no" for an answer. She informed me that she was going to send several samples anyway (she prepared me to receive her product/proposal). When they arrived, I took them out of the package and was pleasantly surprised to see none of them had broken during shipment. They were indeed beautiful, and the Guardian Angel Feather Ornament had a deeply moving verse about the origin of the feather. I quickly thought that I could expand on her product line, and perhaps—as a writer—I could put together an even more impactful poem to accompany the ornaments.

I wrote Marianne another e-mail, let her know that the ornaments had arrived safely, thanked her, and said I would see what I could do. I downloaded the pictures of the ornaments from her website, added them to our site, and took a few on the road with me for back-of-the-room sales as I traveled the country presenting programs for cancer patients. A few of her ornaments sold, none of them broke, and I kind of forgot about them until one special day.

Two weeks before Christmas that year, I was asked to be on our local NBC affiliate to talk about holiday gift ideas for cancer patients. This was the

Saturday morning talk show—a prime ratings period—and I'd have about 2 to 3 minutes with the two hosts. I arrived early and set up a fabulous array of products: books, tapes, stuffed animals, and jewelry items.

Almost as an afterthought, I brought several of Marianne's ornaments with me. As the hosts were oohing and aahing over everything on the table, I instinctively grabbed the Guardian Angel Feather Ornament—it being the holidays—and held it up, telling its story:

We all have a guardian angel up in heaven. Yours has dropped a feather to the ground to let you know she's thinking of you.

I've been told that the way the studio lighting hit the ornament made it appear as if it had indeed been touched by an angel—it sparkled, twirled, and shined. Before the words were out of my mouth, the telephone lines at The Cancer Club started ringing off the hook. The order operators couldn't keep up with the calls. Some determined customers, unable to get through, actually looked our address up on the station's website and began driving over to our office. Within a matter of minutes, we sold out the small supply we had on hand. Confident that Marianne would happily ship us more, we took every order that came our way. Within 2 hours we had sold more than 1,000 ornaments. We continued to fill orders up until the day before Christmas, and we've been selling them ever since.

See, it wasn't that Marianne had done anything *wrong* with the way she was presenting her ornaments. It's just that people couldn't see the entire product. They didn't realize the significance of the poem or grasp that this was the "I have to have that" (IHTHT) pet rock of the moment. Just like a clotheshorse, appearance is king.

In retrospect, it was Marianne's persistence on behalf of her product that made this happen. She didn't accept my first "no" as a final "no." She persevered, informed me she was sending samples, and sent me her product to increase its likelihood of being introduced to others who might appreciate and buy it. And that's exactly what happened. I share this story because the way we package and present products can be the difference between selling 500 pieces or selling 500,000.

Two great retail examples demonstrate the enormous role that design and packaging can play, even in two seemingly mundane products: the MP3 player and the vacuum cleaner. Relying on remarkable packaging—making each iPod look like a precious gift—Apple has come to dominate the MP3 player market with a merely good product. The design and brand building have taken it to its remarkable level.

Similarly, the Oreck vacuum cleaner and its success shows that even a everyday household cleaning product can transform its industry with unique and superior design.

Take the time and spend the money to get your product in the hands of your potential customers—always preparing them for its arrival. If you aren't selling a tangible product, perhaps you can make a short video explaining your service. If you're pitching a charitable cause, you can include any marketing materials your organization has created. If it's something like software, send a sample disk or CD. When they have a chance to see it for themselves—feel it, smell it, taste it, watch it, listen to it—they often will convince themselves of its worthiness.

So what ingredients need to be mixed together to create a knock-your-socks-off impression of you or your company, products, service, or cause?

Only *you* can create awareness of your company, products, and services with clever marketing materials, unique ways to distribute them, and techniques to open doors to customers that will have them saying, "We just have to have it!"

Write a Company/Product/Service/Cause Mission Statement

Write a mission statement that defines the goals and objectives for your company, product, service, or cause. Mission statements need be only three to six sentences long and can contain a certain level of emotion. "This is why we are in business" is the message you are trying to convey.

Why a Marketing Kit?

Time and time again in sales and marketing, we realize a powerful influence: *The visual overwhelms the verbal.* That's why, when expressing this to clients and prospects, we often use phrases such as, "People think with their eyes" and "People hear what they see."

We choose visual clues presented to us by customers and clients that make us appear competent. Visual clues work. We can *listen* to stories of your company's success or remarks from a happy client, but if we can *see* what you have to offer, we're more likely to make a purchase.

The first step toward creating the visual is to put together a knock-your-socks-off marketing kit. Why? Because long after you've left the building, your prospect or client can feel, touch, smell, shake, and *share* a well-put-together marketing kit. Marketing kits have legs.

What's in a Marketing Kit?

Most salespeople are selling the wrong thing. They are selling features; benefits; and, God forbid, price. What should they be selling? Their story and their company's story. Stories are the way the human animal learns. We've seen storytelling all the way back to biblical times.

Why are stories valuable? Because they touch our emotions, capture our hearts, and spur us to take action. So the first thing in your marketing kit should be your company's story: Why did the company get started? What amazing things have happened to past clients and customers as a result of your product or service? Whom will I meet or be allowed to interact with if I join your club or start doing business with your organization? Learn to tell your story, and tell it well.

How Can I Tell My Story?

Create a brochure that covers a broad range of your company's products and services. Who are you? Why did you go into business? How long have you been in business? What makes you unique? What are existing clients and customers saying about you? Who should we contact?

Your brochure or brochures should be brilliant in color and photography. They should capture action, results, and strong testimonials. They can be as simple as a "one sheet"—a glossy $8\frac{1}{2}''$ by $11''$ front and back marketing piece—or as fancy as a trifold. Ideally, you have two brochures: one that does describe your features and benefits and another that tells the story of yourself or your company through the eyes of the employees, volunteers, or committee members.

You can continue to tell your story by including the biography of yourself, your executives, and your founder. Biographies should be more than just the facts; they should be an opportunity to spin a tale about how you or your employees have come to where you are.

The final piece in crafting your story is from the eyes of happy customers. Choose your testimonials wisely, and if you don't have any, go after them. Contact past clients and, if necessary, volunteer to craft the testimonial yourself and submit it to them for approval, editing, and correction. You'll be surprised how many customers will take what you've drafted and change it completely, providing you with an even better and stronger endorsement than you came up with yourself.

What Else?

The actual folder in which you will include your marketing pieces (brochure, biographies, testimonials, business card, etc.) should be custom designed to let your customers and prospects know that you spend money to make money. Investing in a unique pocket folder with a matching envelope should be your top priority. You are competing with hundreds, maybe thousands, of other companies and individuals who do exactly what you do or something similar. When your marketing kit lands on the desk of a prospective CEO, you want him or her to stop what they're doing; notice the package; open it; and say, "Wow! This is amazing."

After my first book was published, we sent boxes of a dozen long-stemmed roses to the top television, newspaper, and radio contacts with one of my trademark cartoons glued to the top of the box, visible under the brilliant pink ribbon: "Mom, more flowers for your breast!" Inside, the book was tucked between the roses.

Finally, in addition to having a coordinated marketing kit with a knock-your-socks-off folder and attention-grabbing envelope in which to deliver it, include any media pieces you or your company have generated about your business. If you get an article in a magazine or newspaper, have it reprinted on the highest possible quality paper, with the name of the magazine/newspaper and date visible as to its currency. Make it a goal to obtain at least one interview or write your own article if necessary and submit it to industry-related publications, blogs, and newsletters (see Chapter 5).

Am I Done Yet?

Marketing kits are a great way to include the complete history of your company or a book or paper written by you or one of your employees as a gift to your prospect. If neither you nor anyone you work with has published anything, choose a book that has meaning to you and that has helped you advance your career. A special note enclosed that says, "Thanks for the opportunity to bid on your business," can make a great first impression.

Again, you want your image to say, "I've invested in you. Now you come invest with me." If you don't want to include a book, create a unique marketing piece that can grab someone's attention. Even your business cards can be used as a promotional piece for your company. When I was with SPAR Marketing, we designed Slinkys that had the words, "We'll bend over backwards for your business" engraved on the product. Years after I had given away hundreds of Slinkys, I would often be sitting in the office of one of my clients and see the Slinky still sitting on their desk or shelf. It was a constant reminder that we really wanted to do business with them.

So much of marketing today is online. If you're selling software, graphic design, or video, for example, or if you just feel that selling online is the right route for your business or your cause, make sure that your online marketing kit and website are as up to date and professional as possible. Today many don't want an actual physical marketing kit. Too bad. They lose a lot of the visual experience. But be prepared by having your entire marketing kit available electronically. And make sure you take the time to print out your marketing kit in its entirety to ensure you approve of how it will look when your customer or prospect downloads it.

The next time you and your staff are hosting a marketing meeting or sales conference, take a good hard look at what you've been sending your customers. If it doesn't knock their socks off, it's time to dial it up and change your image. I'll see you at the bank.

Here's the Real Deal

- The smallest tweak in the way you package your deal can be the difference between success and failure.

- Take the time and spend the money to get your product in the hands of your potential customers.

- Write a mission statement.

- Create a knock-your-socks-off marketing kit.

- Sell your story.

Chapter 3

Let's Customize a Deal

Never change a winning game; always change a losing one.

—Bill Tilden

W e've discussed the importance of packaging your company, product, service, or cause. But perhaps you're an entrepreneur and have created a one-of-a-kind product, or you have a company with a new product introduction. Now you have the opportunity to tap in to an even more lucrative market: the market of product premiums.

Come Closer

Prepare Your Products for Premium Profits

You've published an e-book, recorded a webinar, made a full-length DVD on a subject matter dear to your heart, or created the world's tiniest flashlight. Now what? You can sell your product on the Internet or even through traditional retail outlets such as bookstores and video outlets. The real money to be made, however, is by selling your product for use as a premium to a major corporation or organization.

Webster defines *premium* as "a prize, bonus, or award given as an inducement, as to purchase products, enter competitions initiated by business interests . . . " Some companies or individuals will offer "Buy One, Get One Free" or offer free samples or free trials of their products.

But others will use a different company's product to promote their own. Remember the free scissors I got when I spent $750 on new knives? This is a perfect example of using your product or service to promote another company's product or service. According to Jeff Lonto in the Trading Stamp Store, the first known product premium started in 1793, when a merchant in Sudbury, New Hampshire, started giving out copper tokens when a customer made a purchase.

Examples of product premiums today include everything from getting free ring tones with the purchase of your smartphone, to getting a 60-inch flat-screen TV when you buy a new home, to getting free car washes for a year if you buy a new car. Any product, service, or cause can be applied to another company's product, service, or cause. The result? A win-win-win (your company, the other company, and the consumer).

Write a Product Mission Statement

This time you want to write a mission statement that defines the goals and objectives for your product and how it can be used as a premium by a major corporation. Explain what benefits companies will gain if they use *your* product to promote *their* products or services. Position your product, if possible, for its educational value.

Finding a Target Organization

Target the types of organizations that would be interested in your product to promote theirs. For example, when I wrote my humorous cancer books, I looked at pharmaceutical companies that either manufactured one of the chemotherapy drugs I had taken or one that was manufacturing a drug that could benefit from such a connection. I partnered with Aventis Pharmaceuticals because I had used one of their products, but also with Eisai, that was producing a product to relieve the symptoms of nausea.

In another case, I had produced an exercise video for women recovering from breast cancer surgery. I contacted Schering Oncology Biotech and made my pitch. The company was just releasing a new drug, so my timing was perfect. Schering shrink-wrapped a copy of my video with every order of its drug that shipped to hospitals, oncology clinics, and private clinical practices. The size of the initial order? An impressive 15,000 pieces!

Obtain the name and title of the person within the organization who purchases premiums for the company. Several people may have this responsibility, so it's important to focus on which product the company manufactures or provides that most closely matches your creation. You may want to focus on brand managers, vice presidents of sales, and vice presidents of marketing.

Design a Product Prototype

Design a prototype of your product that will capture your audience's attention and that clearly demonstrates how your product can promote theirs. On a DVD, for example, this may be a custom label, a sticker on the outside packaging that acknowledges the company's newest product, or a custom introduction. In an e-book, it may be customization of the initial page of the book ("This book is being given to you compliments of Aventis Pharmaceuticals"). If possible, package it together with the prospective company's product/service/cause so the company representatives can visualize how this will look to *their* target market. Invest in yourself to create the best possible replication of what your partnership will actually look like.

Write a proposal that clearly states what your product is, the project specifications, the timing in which you could fill a major order, benefits of using your product, pricing, and even a comparison of the competition.

Years ago, there was a wonderful company based in Saegertown, Pennsylvania, called the Charity Bear Company. The company made custom stuffed animals for all different kinds of causes. For years, until it went out of business, the company was a vendor of mine and we sold hundreds of its products through The Cancer Club. But how did the company get my business in the first place? A company representative designed two custom-made bears wearing hats and T-shirts that said, "The Cancer Club" on them. A small gesture turned into a long-term relationship.

Pricing

It is important to lay out several options, including a reduction in price as the purchase quantity gets larger. I suggest orders beginning with 3,000, 5,000, 10,000, or 20,000 pieces. Make sure the premium buyer can make an apples-to-apples comparison of similar products he or she may be evaluating from your competition. It goes without saying that you will be offering a wholesale price, dramatically reduced based on quantity, for your product, service, or cause.

For example, most retailers expect a 50 percent price reduction off the retail value of a product. This means if your invention would cost $10.00 retail, a retailer would typically expect to pay you $5.00 to sell your item in its store. However, when dealing with product premiums, you need to go even lower.

Figure out your total cost per item—from the investment you made to create it to the materials, logo, packaging, and so on. When dealing with product premiums, you want to go as low as you can to still make a profit but price yourself competitively enough to make it affordable. This is not a time to be greedy. Schering Oncology Biotech came back to me with a second order. Its size? A stunning 50,000 additional units.

It's not hard to do the math: Even if you only had a $1 to $2 profit built in for yourself, at 50,000 units, you've made a nice paycheck, gotten national exposure for your product, and created relationships that will hopefully turn into loyals for life (see Chapter 14).

Follow-up

Never send an unsolicited product to a potential buyer without his or her permission. Chances are, if it isn't expected or requested, it will end up in the trash or be given away to anyone who wants it. Call to ensure that the buyer received your package (revisit the deal; see Chapter 13). Discuss what type of time line is reasonable for him or her to review your material.

With the proper timing, persistence, and creativity, you, too, can maximize the potential for your products to become lucrative premiums. But what if you don't have a product or service that can act as a product premium for other companies? Can you still customize your approach?

If you ask an advisor to small businesses, "What is the biggest mistake they make?" you will get an important answer: "They didn't invest enough."

Like businesses of many, this lesson applies powerfully to the Business of One. You have to invest, and you especially have to customize yourself to others. The investments you make demonstrate your confidence in what you offer. The premium prices you pay are literally that: premiums. They are your insurance in your success. Pay more now, and reap more later.

I've tried three things this year that cost a lot of money but paid me back in spades. First, I hired an administrative assistant. In this economy, there are plenty of talented, overqualified people looking for work. How do I know? I found one. Several, actually, but I needed only one.

The woman I hired for $10.00 per hour plus 30 percent commission on sales, resulting in confirmed speaking engagements, is a former public relations (PR)/media mogul. She knows every television and radio personality in my city and is a cancer survivor herself. In her first month, she lined me up to speak with and sign books at hospitals, clinics, and cancer organizations I hadn't done business with in years, if ever.

Why? Because we become stale. We forget to call people in our own backyard. We're too busy doing other things. Take a leap of faith: Invest in people. Talented people can help customize you and your approach.

The second thing I invested in was old-fashioned postcards—5,000 of them, to be exact. The design, postage, and printing were a small fortune. But I needed only one booked event to come out ahead.

What might grab someone's attention?

In honor of Christine's Twenty-Year Anniversary of being a cancer survivor, she has a special offer if you book an event in 2013:

YOU GET TO CHOOSE YOUR FEE! (Expenses not included)

Guess what happened? My phone started ringing off the hook! "Hi, we're a small rural hospital in the Quad Cities, and we've wanted to hire Christine for years but didn't think we could ever afford her. Will she come speak for $X,XXX?"

You bet! So far, 16 new events have been booked at organizations that might never have called me if I hadn't made my special, customized offer. Has it been worth it? Absolutely.

I've sold hundreds of books, gotten spin-off business to higher-paying customers, and added dozens of names to my database. Because I was celebrating a special occasion, I didn't feel I was compromising my fee or my integrity. I was genuinely interested in giving something back.

What's Your Special Occasion? Now Go Out and Do Something About It!

Last thing, I updated my head shot. I know, I know. We all hate that experience. But it had been six years, and to celebrate my anniversary, I decided to grow out my hair. Funny, but after being bald for so long all those years ago, I had kept my hair short ever since chemo. So what happened?

I'd land at my destination, step off the plane, and my host would say, "You don't look anything like your picture!" I heard that enough to know it was time to invest in me. I'm thrilled with my new photographs *and* my new hair.

Customizing *anything*—a presentation, a product sample, a mailing, your appearance—says, "I care about you. I have taken the time to make this all about *you.*"

One of the last things we can almost always customize is price. I'm a firm believer that the higher your price, the higher the perceived value of what it is you're selling. Why would a major corporation want to bring in a $1,000 speaker to address the topic of sales with their international sales force? They're more likely to bring in a $10,000 speaker. Why? Because their perceived value is that the more expensive speaker will know more than their salespeople already know.

This isn't necessarily true, mind you, but value is in the eye—and the mind—of the beholder. On price, we see an increasing migration to either the

30

high or low end—Neiman Marcus and Target are flourishing, while the middle market retailers struggle. Customers are opting for either the best or the best price—just as we see customers mixing $8 Old Navy T-shirts with $900 Prada handbags and nothing in between.

With most products and services, a premium price is an asset. But it is important to provide an underpinning for a premium price. Brand reputation is one, but the real cost of use is another; although a product might be expensive initially, its emphasis on use means that the products ultimately may help your customers reduce their costs, which in turn makes your product even more valuable.

Before you take any steps to pitch and present, have a price range in mind that you—and your superiors, if you have any—are comfortable letting you negotiate without having to stop the sales call to get approval. By having flexibility in pricing, you can demonstrate to others that you care enough about their business to meet them halfway.

Here's the Real Deal

- The real money to be made is by selling your product for use as a product premium to major corporations or organizations.
- Target the types of organizations that would be interested in your product to promote theirs.
- Design a prototype that will capture the buyers' attention and demonstrate how your product can promote theirs.
- Call to ensure the buyers received your product.
- Invest in people and yourself.

Chapter 4

Let's Niche a Deal

The world will never starve for want of wonders.

—Gilbert Keith Chesterton

I n today's competitive business world, within every industry, each sales or marketing opportunity is pursued by hundreds, maybe thousands, of competitors who think they can deliver the best product, service, or message. Our challenge is creating a uniqueness to our business that gives us a competitive edge. We need to produce a one-of-a-kind product or performance that has customers saying, "I have to have that" (IHTHT). This top-of-mind awareness is what I call Niche Notoriety, and it's an integral piece of the puzzle when closing the deal.

A *niche* is a place or position precisely suited to a person's talents or interests. Can you imagine selling something that was custom-closed just for you?

An e-mail arrives. Dr. Vicki Rackner, *CNN* Health Advisor and founder of The Caregivers Club, is asking, "Is there anything I can do to support your work in our fight against cancer?" Moments later, an e-mail comes in from Acharya Sri Khadi Madama, author of *Finding Shangri La: Seven Yoga Principles for Creating Success & Happiness,* recipient of the Jewel of India Award, and TV host of *Yours Truly, Yoga,* asking, "How can we work together?" But the day isn't over. A third e-mail, this time from Dr. Turi, clinical hypnotherapist, astropsychologist, and personal counselor to celebrities such as Ivana Trump and Peter Fonda, has an inquiry: "Can you help me launch a career as a professional speaker on the topic of surviving cancer?"

Add to these eclectic contacts a former president of US Bancorp ("Can you help me launch a career as a professional speaker *and* help me publish my book idea?"), three radio interview requests, six inquiries of my own to come speak, and a proposal to become a regular columnist for a national magazine, and now you have to ask yourself, "What recession?"

Luck? Timing? Sheer coincidence? Or was this a strategy established years ago to perpetuate ongoing business? Creating a niche for yourself—a place where you become the go-to person about that product, service, or cause—is critical to attracting and maintaining customers.

Start with establishing a solid, sustainable personal brand. I speak on the topic of using humor to get through the cancer experience. Who might be interested in that, you wonder? Dr. Rackner, Khadi, Dr. Turi, and a large enough portion of the general population to keep me in business until the day I retire. Because I've spent years focused on establishing a solid, sustainable brand, people and companies worldwide look to me as an expert in my field.

By focusing your resources (time, money, and people) on one primary product, service, or cause and becoming branded with that product, service, or cause, you can attract the type of attention that allows you to not only sell but also consult, teach, write, and train others.

What if you're an employee of a large corporation or organization? Can you still have your own brand? Absolutely! When I sold service contracts for SPAR Marketing, I specialized in the toy industry. What did that do for me *and* for SPAR? It brought us more business because I became the go-to gal who could provide retail services for toys.

Close Enough

John Gill is the uncle to the two children across the street who were the exact ages of my boys. Growing up in the cold Midwest, the four kids entertained themselves for hours playing the usual outdoor games and sports: riding bikes, playing ball, sledding, snowboarding, skiing, and building snow forts.

One day, as dusk started to settle over the city, John watched the boys chase an ice hockey puck up and down the driveway. A lightbulb went off in John's head. Within a matter of weeks, he had developed his first product: Sun Hockey, a brightly flashing, impact- and motion-activated hockey puck that could be used after dark.

John immediately trademarked his product and began selling it to mass merchandisers, to sporting goods stores, and in high school and college arenas. His line expanded quickly to blinking balls for tennis, golf, baseball, and so on. The opportunities were endless.

Then one night John asked his sister how her kids liked the Fireball. She said they liked it fine—but their dog liked it even more! John immediately capitalized on this innovative modification of his invention and expanded his niche by turning his product into a thriving pet toy business. The Pet Fireball grossed $3.5 million dollars in 2002. No one-hit wonder there!

You either have to be first, best, or different.

—Loretta Lynn

John created his own Niche Notoriety by answering these basic questions:

- Can I offer something or have I done something *unique?*
- Is there an area in my field that is *untapped* or *unfulfilled?*
- Do I have much or any *competition?*
- Can I put a *new twist* on my product or service that will appeal to a broad range of people?

For example, in 1994 I was diagnosed with cancer. So were 8 million other people. I offered something unique: using humor and cartoons to inspire cancer patients and caregivers. The "humor and cancer" market was virtually nonexistent when I got started in the business, and I didn't have much competition.

Also, an area in this field was untapped: cartoons. I put a new twist on my subject matter by writing numerous books; creating tapes; producing a newsletter; and putting my cartoons on coffee mugs, T-shirts, and calendars—all focused on the use of therapeutic humor as it relates to the cancer experience. By defining my niche even further, the fact that I'm a breast cancer survivor, I then positioned myself to be uniquely qualified to speak to organizations during National Breast Cancer Awareness Month in October, a niche that generates 20 to 25 speaking engagements during that month alone on an annual basis.

Let's use the world of professional speaking as an example of how to create a niche. I couldn't begin to tell you how many people market themselves as speakers. Note that the National Speakers Association has 2,915 members, which is a reliable and ethical benchmark.

One of the common mistakes made almost universally by everyone is that we want to be all things to all people. For example, if you ask most speakers, "What do you speak about?" their answers can fill a page. "I speak about sales, marketing, team building, leadership, humor in the workplace, relationships, self-esteem, and human resource management." *Whew!*

With that many topics, how can you ever be perceived as an expert in your field? By focusing our resources—and for most of us, this includes our time, money, and people—on one particular area of focus—our niche—we can elevate ourselves to a level of Niche Notoriety and gain industry recognition. In the case of a speaker, for example, he or she would be far better served to say, "I speak on the topic of sales." Ahh . . . now I'm dealing with an expert. You can become even more specialized if you can say, "I speak on the topic of negotiations in the service industry." Are you starting to get the picture?

Why is it important to focus our resources on just one thing? Because our resources are limited. Sooner or later you will realize that it's not oil, gas, water, electricity, or gems that are our most valuable resource. It's time. Think back to when you were a child and you wanted your busy mother or father to read you a story. Mac Anderson, founder of Simple Truths and Successories, and Lance Wubbels wrote a book about it titled *To a Child, Love Is Spelled T.I.M.E.*

Now we're all grown up, and we still want your time. Use it wisely and use it often. Good clients, great friends, and busy children will bask in it and appreciate that you give of yours so freely. Think back on the last person who gave his or her time so generously to you. Then give it like that, only double it. After all, time is free and it is never forgotten.

New Close

So how do we create Niche Notoriety? Take the broad base of your industry and start breaking it down to its lowest level. My brother Greg is a carpenter who lives in Columbia Falls, Montana. When the economy was booming, Greg was busy working for developers building multimillion-dollar homes in the neighboring upscale community of White Fish. For years Greg was riding the wave.

But the economy went south, and so did Greg's business. I visited him one day after the boom had bombed. He hadn't worked for weeks. One day he drove me around White Fish lovingly pointing out all of the houses he'd worked on. But I noticed a trend: Greg was pointing out decks, shutters, stair rails, custom windows, and hardwood floors. I said to him, "Greg, what you really are is a master of fine woodwork. Let's consider a brand that says nothing more than 'Specializes in Fine Woodwork.' Let's create some marketing pieces to promote that side of your business."

Greg and I designed a flyer: *Master of Fine Woodwork.* He had business cards printed on paper that looked and felt like wood. And guess what happened to Greg's business? His phone started ringing off the hook! But guess what else happened to Greg?

It wasn't that Greg couldn't do all of the things that other carpenters do. In fact, he'd go to someone's home to put in new hardwood floors and they'd say to him, "Greg, as long as you're here, can you fix our leaky faucet, rehang some wallpaper, and repair our broken furnace?"

Well, of course Greg can and did do those things for his customers. But he wasn't putting his resources—his time, money, and people—into marketing those *extra* things. Because he had created Niche Notoriety—he had created a brand for himself—he was getting his foot in the door and keeping busy enough. That open door led to lots of business. So much, in fact, that Greg had to subcontract more people. He had become the go-to person for a specific purpose. Ask yourself, "What is my specialty?" (And have one!)

Greg was looking for business in all the wrong places the day he walked into North Valley Ag to buy some dog food for his puppy. A gentleman who has created world-renowned, award-winning Niche Notoriety by specializing in stunning photos of Glacier National Park's famous goats—Sumio Harada—walked in to buy food for his dog, too. He asked the store clerk, "Do you know anyone who can build a carport for me?" Greg, standing right next to him, said, "I can do that for you" and pulled out his custom-made wooden business card. "You're hired!" said Sumio, and together they put together a stunning, natural carport made from trees from Sumio's property.

The key to cultivating a niche is finding a space where you excel over others. To find your own niche, think about:

- What do you or your company know or do best; what do you specialize in?

- A new technique or strategy that could become your area of expertise?

- The latest and greatest technology that no one has seen before?

- The fastest speed of delivery?

If you can position yourself to become your industry leader by creating Niche Notoriety, you will never lack for closing deals. Follow the lead domino theory: Be the first, and all the rest will follow.

What else can you do to create Niche Notoriety? You can start by establishing credibility in your field. Create the eye-catching marketing materials we discussed in Chapter 2. Join industry-related associations and organizations and network like crazy (see Chapter 6). What else?

- **Write a succinct, content-rich article** that can be used in numerous publications. Then sit down and make a list of every organization and association you have ever belonged to: high school, college, sorority or fraternity, church or synagogue, associations, sports affiliations, health clubs, and so on. Send that article to each of their publications departments. Forget spending money on trying to be on *The Today Show*. It's like thinking you'll win the lottery. Print media lives on forever. Why? Because people rip out articles that are of interest to them and keep them . . . in some cases for *years*. We just received an order for The Cancer Club from when our company was located on Limerick Drive. The woman had a copy of an article in her hand. How many years has it been since we were in that location? Eight.

- **Purchase a specialized list of contacts** who are decision makers in your specialty. I purchased a list 16 years ago of directors of oncology at 3,000 cancer centers across the country. I sent them a letter of introduction, a brochure, and a copy of The Cancer Club newsletter. The entire mailing cost me $3,000, but I got 16 paid speaking engagements out of it initially, which more than covered the cost of the investment, in addition to hundreds of book orders and newsletter subscribers. I don't have to keep the names up to date (because I simply address the mailing to "Director of Oncology"), and still use that list for quarterly mailings.

- **Create products** in your industry that can be used as product premiums for larger corporations that sell their products or give away products in your same industry. For example, I recently spoke in Carrollton, Georgia, on behalf of a cancer center. The director of the center asked me if I had a tape of my speech. I told him I'd get one. The next time I spoke, I taped my speech. I've sold thousands of copies.

When I was first starting out positioning myself as an author of books about using humor to get through the cancer experience, I attended a weekend conference hosted by Jack Canfield and Mark Victor Hansen of the *Chicken Soup* series. I noticed that, at every break, dozens of people would line up to have Mark and Jack autograph the books they had just purchased.

I took a different approach. When I got up to the front of the line, I gave Jack and Mark copies of *my* books and explained to them that I was speaking and writing on the topic of using humor to get through the cancer experience.

They both looked at me in amazement and thanked me for *my* books. When I got back home following the conference, I wrote them each a thank-you note for the knowledge I had learned from them and reminded them of our meeting and my books. Lo and behold, I got a handwritten postcard from Jack Canfield.

Thanks for all the stuff you sent me. You are doing great work.

I am inspired by your message.

Love to you, Jack

I contacted Jack again. "Jack, may I use the words you sent me on my marketing materials and as a testimonial in my upcoming book?" He agreed. I thought to myself, "It's so simple [ISS] that I should try contacting other celebrities and experts in my field." And I have done that ever since. Monty Hall—producer, actor, singer, sportscaster, and best known as host of the television game show *Let's Make a Deal*—was only a phone call away!

It's a matter of taking the time to reach out, asking for what it is that you are seeking, and following up to ensure success.

What else can you do to create Niche Notoriety and let people know you exist? The Internet and social media have made it extremely easy to blast out news about you and your niche. To facilitate this process, you can purchase lists of targeted customers, write a newsletter, and send out a mass mailing to your database. You can hire telemarketers to make phone calls using pre-approved lists. Anything you can do to create awareness of your expertise will benefit you and your company. The next chapter offers several suggestions about ways to publicize your niche through the use of media.

Celebrities have certainly learned how to create Niche Notoriety. You can establish credibility in your niche by following the Taylor Swift theory: Build it, and they will come. So tightly has she marketed herself and her niche (lovelorn songs about romances gone bad) that her most recent album release, "Red," charted first-week sales of 1.21 million copies, according to Nielsen SoundScan. That is the biggest first-week figure in more than a decade.

What went into the Taylor Swift theory? The 23-year-old knows the power of building her brand. Every company and every individual benefits today from brand building; the trend is unmistakable. Yahoo! demonstrated it by building a great success around a merely good product. At retail in mutual funds, we see that the three best-known mutual fund brands (Fidelity, Janus, and Vanguard) also are the three biggest sellers—even when their performance among all mutual funds ranked second, thirty-fifth, and thirty-eighth. In a world of so many competitive alternatives, Taylor Swift benefits from continuing to build her brand awareness and reputation. Brands are shortcuts that customers and clients use to make and justify their choices.

The importance of building a brand is further demonstrated by the essential failure of generic products at retail. It was assumed that an unbranded product with an exceptional price—a low price made possible by the absence of advertising and marketing costs—would command a significant market. But not even low-income families chose generic products; in fact, many low-income families showed a greater preference for branded products than did middle-income families.

Brands work.

What else did the Taylor Swift theory prove? That she looked for business in all the wrong places. When for decades albums were something you bought in record stores, Swift is selling CDs with Keds "Red" sneakers at Target or with a large pepperoni pizza at Papa John's. Along with the pizza, you get her image on the pizza box!

So you've seen the benefit of drilling down—down far enough to become the go-to person in your industry or trade. Niche Notoriety translates into sales. But what could be the pratfalls and dilemmas of creating Niche Notoriety?

You get so well known, or your product becomes so popular, that you can't fulfill the demand. Every year for National Cancer Survivors Day (the first Sunday in June), I get seven or eight requests to speak. I can be in only one place at one time. We've seen this happen to the newest iPhone, Halo video game, and gas.

Changing Your Niche

Your niche may go away or change. Think fax machines, bookstores, video outlets, and landlines.

You can also personally become disinterested in your niche. Or you get sick or have a crisis during your company or product's peak performance period. These are all real possibilities, and they could happen to you.

But in the end, having Niche Notoriety will only elevate you to new opportunities, better and stronger connections, and the knowledge that you have the tools to do it again. It helps to be able to capitalize on your niche by not creating a one-hit wonder. John Gill saw beyond his first glow-in-the-dark hockey puck. I used the knowledge I had gained by developing The Cancer Club to develop a company called Divorcing Divas and wrote a humorous cartoon book about the divorce experience.

It's been almost 20 years since I established myself as an expert in the field of therapeutic humor. And because I've followed all of the steps I've outlined in this chapter, just today I was contacted by the *Chicago Tribune* to be interviewed for a story on the power of humor during the cancer journey. Why? Because 20 years ago I established myself as an expert in my field.

Dr. Rackner and I have done business together, and proposals are on the table to Khandi, Dr. Turi, and the former chief executive officer. Speeches have been booked, articles have been written, and the radio interviews have gone extremely well, thank you very much. But I'm still heading out the door with my golf clubs on my back because I learned long ago: Build it, and they will come. Build your Niche Notoriety—your personal brand—and come join me on the back nine.

Here's the Real Deal

- Establish a solid, sustainable personal brand.

- Focus your resources—time, money, and people—on one area of expertise to build Niche Notoriety.

- Follow the lead domino theory: Be the first, and all the rest will follow.

- Establish credibility by following the Taylor Swift theory: Build it, and they will come.

Chapter 5

Let's Market a Deal

Getting ready to get ready gets you nowhere. It's organization and follow-through that get results.

—H. James Zinger

Webster defines *marketing* as "the ability to attract a buyer if offered for sale." What exactly is it you are trying to sell—a service, a product, a concept, or an idea? Whatever it is, it's up to you to attract the buyer.

I think this is the most exciting and fun part of our job.

Marketing involves knowledge . . . of your product, market, and competition. Once you've learned everything you can about these three areas, you can identify the tools necessary to separate yourself from the pack. One way to separate yourself from the pack is to look for business in all the *wrong* places and leave no "store" unturned. Here's an example.

Close Encounter

Running errands on a weekend afternoon, I stood in line at my neighborhood FedEx store, dressed casually in sweatpants and wearing no makeup. Waiting to pay, I couldn't help but notice the letterhead on the paperwork of the gentleman standing in front of me, which read, "Minnesota Hospice Organization Annual Convention."

My first thought was, "What a great potential speaking opportunity." I wanted to introduce myself, but my second thought was that I wasn't dressed professionally and it was a Sunday afternoon; maybe he didn't want to be bothered. So I asked myself the question that drives my ability to close deals: "What is the *worst* thing that can happen to me here?"

The worst thing that could happen was he would cut our conversation short and decide not to speak to me. The best thing that could happen was we'd make a rewarding win-win-win connection. I decided to speak up to give the win-win-win a chance.

"Excuse me, sir," I started. "I couldn't help but notice your materials. I'm a professional speaker and one of my topics is on the use of using humor to overcome life's adversities. Does your organization use outside speakers for its convention?"

"Why, yes, we do, and that sounds like an interesting topic. Of course, we already have all our speakers lined up for this particular convention, but maybe at some point in the future." He glanced off to the counter where the clerk was ready to take his order.

"I understand completely," I said, "My name is Christine Clifford, and if you have a moment, I'd love to give you a little information about the services I provide."

"Great," he responded. "I'll catch up with you in a few minutes."

That simple question opened the door to a new venue of prospects and markets I had never even thought of contacting—end of life. The focus for my topic had always been with hospitals, women's expos, and charitable organizations. When the gentleman left the counter, we reconnected to finish our conversation.

"My name is Jim," he responded. "I'm in a clerical position with our organization. Sorry, but I really can't help you with speaking opportunities—that's not my department."

Handing him my card, I asked, "Jim, would you happen to know who exactly would be responsible at your organization? I'd love to contact him or her prior to your next convention."

He graciously gave me the name and number of their executive director. Monday afternoon I phoned the office and explained the situation and my speaking services. Within six months, I was booked as the closing keynote speaker for their spring Team Management and Leadership Development Conference. Luck? Timing? I like to think of it as looking for business in all the wrong places, and it's a key element to separating yourself from your competition. Next time you run into someone who is somehow associated with your target audience, don't let that opportunity slip away. Even if the person you meet is not the decision maker, he or she may be able to refer you to the person who is.

Too often we chase the same customers everyone else is chasing. Marketing involves having your antennae up all the time. It means putting out feelers for potential customers, places, or things that might offer business you never even dreamed you could have. It means pursuing leads—even when they initially appear to be long shots. It would never have occurred to me to look for business in a print shop. But if I hadn't had my feelers out, I would have missed out on a great business opportunity.

That particular Minnesota Hospice Convention has long been over, but I was able to further capitalize on that chance meeting in the print shop. After addressing their Team Management and Leadership Development Conference and receiving high ratings, I asked the executive director if he would be comfortable writing a letter of recommendation and providing me with a list of the other 49 state directors. I also asked permission to use his name in a query letter. The result? I've had the opportunity to speak at three to four state hospice conventions every year since. I keep my share of the bargain by doing my best to deliver an outstanding presentation each time. All this is possible because I happened to look over someone's shoulder at a print shop and followed up on the resulting referral.

The moral of this story? Is it that the next time you're standing in line, you should be sure to hobnob with the clientele? No, although that's a good idea. It's that business opportunities are everywhere, waiting for you when you're out on a walk, in the doctor's office, or eating at a restaurant. Marketing is an everyday, everywhere affair. Don't wait for the annual trade show or sales meeting. Be willing to talk to strangers. You never know who might be hiding in all the wrong places.

Stepping into an elevator of a hotel in San Antonio, Texas, I glanced at the name tag of a woman already inside: Kathryn McKenzie, Oncology Program Manager, Public Relations & Ally Development Public Affairs, AstraZeneca. Then I did what all of us have done at one time or another: I hesitated. "Should I, shouldn't I?" I thought frantically as we climbed toward the hotel lobby. I took a deep breath and decided, "What's the *worst* thing that can happen to me here?"

"Ms. McKenzie? My name is Christine Clifford, and I couldn't help but notice your name tag and your position with AstraZeneca. I'm a cancer survivor and the author of several books on using humor to get through the cancer experience. I just thought I'd thank you for all the work AstraZeneca is doing to save the lives of cancer patients."

Bingo! It just so happened that Kate—as she asked me to call her—was personally responsible for putting together a program for her company to be called Visions of Hope Community Speakers Program. They were going to bring well-recognized patients, advocates, and key thought leaders in the field of breast cancer to local communities to educate the public on this disease and provide inspiration.

Kate had heard of me and my work because I had already created Niche Notoriety. And because I took that risk—I looked for business in an elevator and then took advantage of it by introducing myself—for two years I worked with Kate and their wonderful program. Thanks, Kate, for being in that elevator that day.

Use the Media to Gain Notoriety and Grow Your Business

How else can you market your business? Do you ever think to yourself, "If I could only get the *right* piece of exposure for our company [or our cause, our product, or our service], we could double our business, sell a million pieces, and exceed our expectations?"

Only the media has the ability to make you or your company a star overnight. You may not sell a million pieces of product or make a million presentations in a lifetime, but the use of the media *can* and *will* draw valuable and necessary attention to you and your message. Make it a goal to get one piece of exposure.

Media has been described as "an ancient country in NW Iran, which flourished in mid 7th century B.C., conquered Assyria, and destroyed Ninevah . . . or the middle membrane of a blood or lymph vessel." In other words, the media will either conquer and destroy you, or give you a very large headache! We've certainly seen that happen with hundreds of celebrities and captains of commerce.

The other definition, however, is that *media* is "a substance or means through which something acts or gets done; a source of news and information." Forms of media include television, radio, print (newspapers, magazines, periodicals, blogs, newsletters, etc.), and the Internet. Media can be local, national, or international, but the best place to start is at home. Make it a goal to get one piece of local media exposure. How do you do that? Read on.

Create a Need for Media Consideration

Ask yourself the following four questions:

- Do we offer something unique?
- Is there an area in our field that is untapped/unfulfilled?
- Can we put a new twist on our subject matter that will appeal to a broad range of people?
- Do we have much competition?

If you can answer "yes" to the first three and "no" to the fourth, you may have something that would be of interest to the media. The media will rarely go out on a limb to feature someone who is relatively unknown unless you are unique, have passion, or spin a new twist on your subject matter. Hometown papers, local radio, and so on, however, are hungry for hometown stories, whereas the national media is more inclined to look for an expert while still wanting to be first to break the news.

We've talked in previous chapters about the importance of establishing credibility in your field by designing professional marketing materials, joining industry-related associations and organizations, writing articles for newsletters, blogs, and magazines that demonstrate your area of expertise in your field, and collecting testimonials and letters of commendation from other experts in your field. So let's assume you've done that. Now how do you get the world to sit up and pay attention?

Grab the Media's Attention

There are seven ways to get the media's attention.

Pure Luck In 1995 I was in the middle of chemotherapy, and as a way of keeping my mind off my situation, I had started to draw cartoons about my cancer experience. I carried them with me wherever I went so that if I had a down moment or started to feel sorry for myself, I could pull them out for a good laugh.

I was still calling on Kmart Corporation in Detroit for SPAR Marketing, and one day after making sales calls, I boarded a plane to fly home to Minneapolis. As I sat down, I realized that the woman sitting next to me was none other than Pat Miles, our local NBC news anchor in Minnesota and a celebrity in her own right. We had met before, and as we settled in and started talking, she told me how sorry she was to learn that I had been battling cancer. She went on to share with me that she had lost her only sister to colon cancer at the age of 35.

There are a lot of theories about luck, but one definition I read many years ago was that *luck* is "when preparation meets opportunity." I pulled my cartoons out of my briefcase and showed them to Pat.

Pat got very excited and said, "We need to do a story about this! I'll have our health care producer get in touch with you, Christine." After about a week

I got a call from Pat. "Christine, I've decided to do this story myself. When can we come interview you?"

That chance seating next to Pat was certainly lucky. But if I hadn't had my cartoons with me and had simply tried to explain to her that I was drawing cartoons, I'm confident nothing would have come from that experience. Instead, KARE 11 (NBC) ended up doing a 6-minute piece on the 10:00 PM news. At the end of the piece, they posted a phone number for The Cancer Club. More than 400 phone calls came in to my single telephone line inside my home from people wanting to buy my cartoon book—which hadn't even been published yet! (Word to the wise: Don't ever get publicity before you're ready to handle it.)

Be prepared for luck when it crosses your path. I once spoke for the Inventors Network. After my program, as each attendee came up to me to ask a few questions or generate a few ideas, I'd ask to see his or her invention. Not a single person had brought it! Ideas will never materialize sitting in garages and in desk drawers.

Bouncebacks A bounceback is when someone from one magazine, newspaper, or TV station sees you on another. It turns out that someone from our local newspaper, the Minneapolis *Star Tribune,* saw the piece on KARE 11 that night. The very next day I got a call that a reporter wanted to interview me. The paper ran a two-page, full-color spread on the front page of the Variety section and featured several of my cartoons. The *Star Tribune* was owned by a large national firm that made the article available nationwide to its database of affiliates. Soon the article was running in the *Detroit Press,* the *Chicago Tribune,* and numerous other publications around the country.

The *Star Tribune*'s competition on the other side of the Mississippi, the *St. Paul Pioneer Press,* saw the article in the *Tribune.* A reporter there, too, asked to write an article—and this one was even larger and more colorful. It appeared in the Sunday edition. The paper was also owned by a large conglomerate, so the article popped up in papers all across the country. I was off and running.

Cash Purchases   You can buy media exposure. Companies such as Finn Partners Media Connect (formerly Planned Television Arts), media relations and public relations (PR) companies can get articles about you and your company, product, service, or cause in the news. You can also use services such as PR Newswire or PR Web to distribute press releases online.

Advertise   Services for publicizing your expertise can be purchased through venues such as Radio-TV Interview Report (RTIR) and the Yearbook of Experts, Authorities & Spokespersons or through traditional print, radio, television, and Internet ads.

Free Media Services   Two excellent media services provide free daily leads to reporters, producers, authors, and bloggers. One is HARO (Help A Reporter Out) at www.helpareporter.com, and the other is Reporter Connection at www.reporterconnection.com. Through these two services I have appeared in and/or been interviewed by AmExp OPEN Forum, *Better Homes & Gardens,* the *New York Times,* the *Wall Street Journal,* the *Huffington Post,* and more. HARO is delivered three times per day, and Reporter Connection is delivered twice daily.

Hard Work   Write your own press releases; post on Twitter, Facebook, and LinkedIn; call and e-mail media contacts; and post videos on YouTube. Start building a list of media contacts and work your list whenever something new or different happens to you or your company.

When I started Divorcing Divas, a company that hosts all-day educational conferences for people facing divorce, I started contacting all of the local magazines and community periodicals across the state. Our first year we found enormous success because we were new and different. In subsequent years, however, I learned that we needed to put a new twist on our subject matter. So I dug deep to find a speaker, volunteer, committee member, sponsor, or vendor from each local city so I could customize my pitch. "Although our event is being held in St. Louis Park," I'd begin explaining, "one of our speakers, Mitch Irwin with Bell Mortgage, is from Woodbury and will be speaking on the subject of financing or refinancing your home during the divorce process. We also have an attendee, Bonnie Bakken from Woodbury, who has attended our event three times. May I put you in touch with them for an interview?"

We went from having a neighborhood magazine—*Woodbury Magazine*—that probably would never have given our event coverage to doing a feature story. Dig deep and work hard to get more media attention.

Referrals   The first rule is to ask for referrals. If you are a guest on a radio show or television network, ask the producer who booked you on the show if there are other shows within that network that he or she thinks could benefit from having you as a guest. Ask your radio show hosts to post positive reviews of you on the BitBoard, a sharing network of talented and creative guests and interviews.

The most important piece of advice I can offer if you do secure an interview and your contact asks you to forward your information is to mark any package you send with big, bold letters directly on the box saying, "REQUESTED MATERIAL." That way, your box can easily be segregated from the hundreds of unsolicited materials that cross your contact's desks every day.

If one media outlet features you, others will follow. Media is like a rubber ball—it comes bouncing back to you.

Where to Start

Set a goal of what type of media you want (print, television, radio, online, etc.). Start at the very lowest level: your local television stations, newspapers, magazines, and community papers. Send press releases and/or articles you've written to your alma mater, hometown newspaper, health club newsletter, church or synagogue, or any associations or organizations that you are a member of and that publish a blog or newsletter.

Your press releases should be dated with the current date and should explain the who, what, why, where, and how of your company, product, service, or cause; how you got started; and what is new and exciting. The headline of your press release must capture the producer's attention. If you don't know how to write a press release or have never seen one, hire a PR firm or consultant to help you draft your first one.

Keep track of your media for the big players: Create a log of your media hits. Post articles and appearances on the home page of your website under the title "Media Highlights." By posting your media hits on your website, your search engine optimization will increase and improve.

What to Do If You Get It

Prepare   Know exactly what you want to say. If possible, ask the host who is going to interview you if you can forward your top-10 questions you'd like to be asked. Take control of your interview by making sure you mention your website or the name of your product, event, or company as many times as possible. I've found the hard way that often you can be a guest for up to 3 minutes on a television show, but if I didn't mention the title of my new book or how people could get ahold of it on our website, the hosts often skipped over this vital information.

Never go to an interview blind. If you aren't familiar with the hosts or the show that you are going to be a guest on, make the time to watch or listen for at least a week in advance. Discover what the host seems drawn to and what other products, services, and causes he or she promotes. Ask if you can bring props or give away free samples of your product to the first five people who contact the station. Treat an appearance on radio or television the way you'd treat a job interview: Always be prepared.

Primp   Dress appropriately for your interview and get your makeup professionally done, your hair cut, your mustache trimmed, your eyebrows waxed—whatever you need to do to look your best. If you're talking about gardening or outdoor sports, you can dress more casually. If you're talking about an upcoming benefit or fund-raiser, you want to dress in business attire. Ask the producer what is expected of you.

Bring along extra face powder. Guys—this means you, too! Even sitting in the green room waiting to go on air can cause anxiety, which may lead to perspiration on your face and forehead. Don't be shy about using the restroom to check yourself out in the mirror one last time before you go live.

Practice   Role-play with friends and family. How do you get good at something? Practice, practice, practice. Draft your list of 10 questions and have someone ask you those questions. Take time to craft succinct yet factual answers to the questions. If possible, have someone record your answers so you can critique them ahead of time.

Project Effectively   Exude confidence, use voice control, and watch your body language. If possible, hire a media coach to help you learn to project effectively. When I first started publicly speaking, I didn't realize it but I had a tendency at the end of every sentence to make a slight "tsk" sound with my tongue. A media coach I hired pointed it out to me, and I was able to eliminate it immediately from my sentences. But if no one had ever told me I was doing it, I'd still be tsking my way around the globe!

Act on It Once You've Had It

So you appeared on your local ABC affiliate with a great story about your newest invention. What's left?

Write Thank-You Notes   Handwritten notes of thanks are still the best, but at a minimum, send an e-mail thanking the hosts and producers for having you on the show. Mention that you hope they'll keep you in mind for future shows that focus on your subject matter.

Reprint Your Articles Professional services can make reprints on beautiful, glossy paper for any articles that appear in most magazines and periodicals. Make duplicates of any videos; make recordings of any radio interviews. Bring your own DVD or CD to the studio and ask if they'll burn you a copy of your appearance. Make sure you obtain permission from the station or publisher to use the article or show on your website or in your marketing kits. Today, most stations and producers are thrilled if you want to share your interviews on your social media and/or website, but again, make sure you have permission and that you provide the proper credit.

Send It to Everyone You Know Send out copies of articles you have written or appear in to members of your family, your friends, and any associations or organizations to which you belong. You never know who might pass it on to someone else who can end up getting you additional coverage. Besides, it helps to spread the word.

Do Targeted Mailings to Other Media Contacts With Your Own Press Release Although most media outlets want to be the first to have you, you can cross-promote by sending an article you've written for a magazine to all the local television stations. You can send a video you've recorded of a segment you did on television to a major magazine to position you as an expert in your field—ready, willing, and able to write an article for their publication.

Trade It With Others Who Have Similar Media Contacts Who Can Help You Grow Your Business If you have colleagues, board members, or neighbors who have appeared in your local media, ask them if you can trade them the names and contact information for one of your contacts. That way you are not having to cold-call a media contact. You can start the conversation with, "One of our board members, Linda Jennings, gave me your name and contact information as a person who may be interested in having me on your show." Remember: A "warm" call is always better than a cold call.

Keep the Momentum Going

You can always build your own media event and invite the press. Make sure you obtain an original copy, reprint, or tape and dissect it. Learn from your mistakes. Read and study the media. Know what's happening in your field that is newsworthy.

So Now I'm a Star?

Accept each media event at face value and be grateful for the exposure and publicity. Don't expect recognition—getting media attention and consideration is a constant battle. And last but not least: Remain humble. Even the biggest stars have to change diapers, let the cat out, and take out the trash. I'll see you in the news!

Here's the Real Deal

- Look for business in all the wrong places; leave no "store" unturned.

- Marketing is an everyday, everywhere affair.

- Make it a goal to get one piece of media exposure.

- Create a need for media consideration.

- Act on media once you get it. It's like a rubber ball—it comes bouncing back to you.

Chapter 6

Let's Connect a Deal

If a man does not make new acquaintances, as he advances through life, he will soon find himself left alone.

—Samuel Johnson

D o you know someone who seems to know *everybody?* Have you ever wondered, "How do they meet all those people?" Regardless of your expertise or specialty, connecting with the right people can propel your career faster than almost anything else besides the media.

One Degree of Separation

Six degrees of separation is five too many. Cultivate enough clients, friends, relatives, and acquaintances that it would take you only one phone call to make the connection that will solve your problem, create a new lead, or get you a new client. You've all heard since childhood, "Make new friends, but keep the old." Make enough friends, and you'll never be at a loss for anything—business or otherwise.

There are several ways to make mutually productive connections. All of them work, and each has advantages and disadvantages.

Let's look at the ways we can connect with someone we want to meet:

- Start from the bottom, networking our way up that person's corporate ladder.

- Start at the top by going straight to the source.

- Position ourselves to be in the right place at the right time.

- Connect from the inside out by expanding our network of contacts and industries.

- Connect from the outside in, working our way into a company or individual's "inner circle." This is what is known as old-fashioned cold calling, and although it's the most difficult way to obtain business, it does work if you position yourself correctly to close the deal.

Here is what is involved to start from the bottom up. Let's say you have been dying to meet someone you hope can open doors for your product, service, or cause. Perhaps by getting to know that person, you may be able to advance your career. But you have no current relationship with that individual or with anyone at his or her company. Where do you begin?

Start asking questions of others who you know are already doing business with that person or company. Even if it's one of your competitors, it never hurts to ask, "How's business?" It's human nature for people to want to make it appear as if business is booming. Listen carefully while this individual goes into detail about what's working well for him or her. You may learn that the person you want to meet is an avid golfer, stamp collector, or musician. You could start the conversation by saying, "Ed, I heard you landed the Fix-It Tool Company account. Way to go! I understand their president, Mike, is an avid fisherman."

Before you know it, Ed may say, "Yup, I did get that account. But Mike isn't an avid fisherman—he's a marathon runner." Hmmm. Make a note of this tiny morsel of information. It could be just the door opener you need to make a connection with Mike at some point in the future.

Sometimes it seems impossible to make contact with an executive, celebrity, or expert in your field due to that person's high visibility, gatekeeper, and busy schedule. Should you give up on trying to connect? Not at all. Rather, start by making contact with a person who is lower on that individual's corporate totem pole. Here's an example:

Close Up

When I began writing my first book, one of my top priorities was to get a meeting with Mr. Harvey Mackay, CPAE, chief executive officer (CEO) of the Mackay Envelope Company and author of *Swim With the Sharks Without Being Eaten Alive*. Why Harvey? He's been enormously successful in the publishing industry, and at the time, he had a book on the *New York Times* list of best sellers for more than 52 weeks. The "King of the Rolodex" was well connected, was knowledgeable, and lived in my hometown. Did he know me? No.

So I contacted friends and associates who knew Harvey through golf or the media. I even asked a doctor friend of mine who had said in a passing conversation that he knew the president of Harvey's company. I asked each of them to call, write, or e-mail on my behalf to see if Harvey would take a phone call from me. The conversations would sound something like this: "Jamie, I understand that you know Harvey Mackay from your golf club. I have been trying to get through to him to discuss a book I am writing, and he hasn't taken my calls. I know how busy he is, and I'm wondering, do you know Harvey well enough to call him on my behalf and see if he'll take my phone call?"

My philosophy is it never hurts to ask. The worst thing Jamie could say was, "I don't feel comfortable doing that," or "I don't know him well enough." If that had been Jamie's response, I would have backed off. I don't want to pressure my friends; I always want our relationship to be one of trust and respect. However, Jamie might voluntarily go to bat for me based on the favors I've done for him over the years. He might say, "I don't know him that well, but my friend Karen knows him really well. Let me give her a call."

Through those types of contacts and referrals, I secured an appointment to get in the door. I met Harvey's assistant, Greg Bailey. Greg and I hit it off and had several things in common. His sister had fought breast cancer, and I made sure he received an autographed copy of my book *Not Now . . . I'm Having a No Hair Day!* (which is a way of Perk-O-Lating the deal; see Chapter 9).

Friends' phone calls also resulted in an appointment for breakfast with the president of Harvey's firm, Scott Mitchell. I anticipated that there was one "gift" that would have special importance to Harvey and his right-hand man Scott. On the day of my meeting with Scott, I brought a list of all of my contacts. That list of qualified buyers was 30 pages long and included names, addresses, and phone numbers. I also gave Scott and his sales team permission to use my name when contacting these individuals. This was a win-win-win because I knew Scott's company operated with the utmost quality and integrity. Therefore it was a win for my associates to learn more about a company that could provide them with top-notch stationery. It was a win for Scott and his sales team because, using my name, they now had warm access (versus a cold call) to hundreds of new potential clients. It was certainly a win for me because I now had entrée to Harvey and a possible endorsement.

Connecting my way through Harvey's web of professional and personal relationships landed me a personal appointment with him and several others since. It always helps to know the receptionist, secretaries, and administrative personnel—the gatekeepers—who, once they know you by name, can hand you the key to the head office. The advantages of this approach, closing from the bottom up, will pay off time and again because you've created solid relationships with even more individuals in that person's inner circle. The disadvantages? It will definitely take longer and may require several appointments with associates before you reach your targeted individual.

Our belief at the beginning of a doubtful undertaking is the one thing that insures the successful outcome of our venture.

—William James

Close Down

Let's look now at the opposite approach: from the top down by going straight to the person you want to meet. This can be a scary proposition because we're afraid this person we've wanted to meet will abruptly brush us off. It's made us gun-shy. We're more likely to be successful if we find a compelling way to open the conversation that brings him or her into our circle of friendship.

Have you ever looked across a crowded room only to spot a respected icon or sought-after CEO surrounded by a mob of eager individuals? "If only I could have 10 minutes with him," you think as you stare wistfully. Find an area of commonality, preferably through a reference from someone who already knows that individual. How deep do you need to dig to find a connection? You can't dig deeply enough.

When trying to connect with people like this, research where they grew up; which high school they attended; whether they went to college; if so, whether they were active in any campus organizations, fraternities, or sororities; what they did after college; whether they play sports; where they've worked; where they live now; whether they are married or have children; if so, what sports their children play; and what charitable organizations they support? Get the picture? Find something that you have in common so that when you finally have the opportunity to meet, you can start with the words, "I understand your son is attending the University of Denver. I went to college there in the '70s. Gosh, has that campus changed a lot over the years!"

Or muster up your courage and approach the key contact head-on with a statement such as, "Hello, my name is Mike Smith. Our mutual friend, Janet Krammer, felt that if I could have 5 minutes of your time, you might find the work I am doing of interest to you and your corporation."

Keep your request small. Don't ask for an hour of their time. Ask for 5 minutes so it's relatively risk-free and it's easy for them to say "yes." If you approach an expert in your field with this type of introduction, the worst thing that can happen is that they say, "No, thank you." Your ego may be bruised and you may feel a twinge of rejection, but trust me, there will be no permanent damage.

The best outcome, however, is that the person will give you 10 or 20 minutes. And, if you've prepared your pitch so it clearly and compellingly meets this individual's needs, you may even get more time and end up closing a deal.

Next time you're at an industry-related event, make it a point to introduce yourself to the experts and offer to become a resource for them. Establishing relationships with experts can open new doors of opportunity, knowledge, and revenues. How do you do this? A friend and fellow speaker approaches best-selling authors at writers' conferences, makes a specific compliment about their latest work, and lets them know she'll be glad to help out at one of their book signings when they're in her area. She's so friendly; she's made some marvelous connections this way and has also received impressive testimonials from well-known authors for her books.

Perfect Close

One of the best ways to create connections is to plan to be in the right place at the right time. *Positioning* is defined as "intentionally placing yourself wherever luck is most likely to happen." If there is someone you would like to meet—someone who you think could enhance your success—meeting that person is as straightforward as researching the places he or she frequents, the types of conventions he or she attends, and his or her hobbies and outside interests. Make it a point to attend those places and conventions and participate in the same hobbies. Connections occasionally happen by coincidence (e.g., my FedEx store visit in Chapter 5), but it's more effective to strategize how you can be in the same place at the same time so that you're exponentially increasing the likelihood of meeting who you want to meet. The following story illustrates how this can involve time, effort, and yes, investment. When done right, however, it is well worth it.

Calling on Kmart Corporation for years, I met many staff members throughout their corporate headquarters from the receptionists at both the front and the back door lobbies, the clerks in shipping and receiving, the accountants, marketing personnel, and almost every buyer in the building. There was one individual I'd never had the opportunity to meet—the president, Joe Antonini.

I always try to stay current on the news about my customers; it's a key component to staying up to date about their needs, which is a big part of providing the quality services that keeps customers loyal. I learned through the

Detroit newspapers that Joe was heavily involved in philanthropic causes throughout the Detroit community. One week an article announced that he was going to be honored for his philanthropy at a fund-raising dinner hosted by B'nai B'rith.

I realized that if I wanted to meet this man, this may be my only chance. He was guaranteed to be there that night for the entire evening. I had a decision to make: I could buy an inexpensive ticket, but that would mean I was seated in the back of the room, far away from the head table. If I was serious about connecting with Mr. Antonini, I would have to invest the money to buy the most expensive ticket, which is why I plunked down $500 for the opportunity to sit at Table 1. I went by myself and remember arriving at the event feeling alone, rather intimidated, and very out of place.

I didn't know anyone there. I mingled a bit during the reception; however, I couldn't wait to be seated for dinner. And, just as I had hoped, I was seated next to Joe Antonini and his wife. I could hardly contain my excitement; however, I didn't want to plunge in and hog the conversational ball. No one appreciates being collared or hard sold at these social events. So I bided my time and enjoyed the dinner discussion, listening to the chitchat swirling around the table and adding something only when I felt it had value for everyone at the table. After a while, the conversation came full circle back to me. "What do you do, Christine?" asked someone.

I said that I was in sales and that, interestingly enough, Kmart was one of my clients, and I had been a longtime admirer of Joe's management style. Of course, that lead-in caught Joe's attention, and we started a fascinating conversation about his work and mine. The rest, as they say, is history. Not long after that introduction, I closed my first million-dollar contract . . . with Kmart Corporation. Thanks, Joe.

Every once in a while after sharing that story from the platform, an audience member will speak up and say, "$500 for dinner? I would *never* pay that much money for a meal." I try to delicately point out that a million-dollar contract for a $500 investment was a nice return on investment!

Furthermore, I probably never would have met Joe if I hadn't taken that rather bold initiative. The question is, as the late Johnny Carson would have asked, "How *much* do you want to meet this particular individual?"

Let's summarize what happened here, why I think that was time and money well spent, and why this step-by-step strategic approach helped me close a big deal:

1. I targeted exactly who I wanted to meet.

2. I researched the types of places that my target frequented and positioned myself to be in the right place at the right time.

3. It takes money to make money. I didn't want to take any chances, so I purchased the most expensive ticket to ensure that I would be able to get an introduction. The outcome would have been completely different if I had bought a $25 ticket and sat in the back of the room.

4. I put myself in a favorable position by not rudely jumping the gun. I allowed the social interactions to proceed normally. By the time I got the opportunity to introduce myself and talk about my work as a salesperson, I was "embraced" by the group because I had been an enthusiastic listener and diplomatic participant.

You also are capable of creating these chance closings and don't-leave-anything-to-chance closings. Once you set them up, though, it's imperative that you be prepared to act on the connection that was created. Here are five easy steps to keep the positive momentum going:

1. **Send handwritten thank-you notes within 24 hours of your introduction.** Acknowledge the assistance, knowledge, and/or insight the person gave you and remind him or her of your meeting, however brief it may have been. Enclose your business card and say you will call again. Yes, this takes time—about 5 minutes. Is 5 minutes worth a million-dollar deal? Just think about it. When was the last time *you*

received an old-fashioned handwritten note from someone thanking you for your time and attention?

2. **Send your marketing materials and product samples for review.** Don't just send *any* marketing materials or samples, however: Send your very best. I call this a fully loaded media kit—the knock-your-socks-off marketing kit we discussed in Chapter 2. Try to customize the packet of materials with industry-related letters of recommendation, articles from the media relative to that person's industry, and even customized product samples, if possible. Think quality, not quantity.

   Several years ago, I mentioned to a friend that I was struggling with a business-related speech I was working on. She mentioned that a fellow speaker and author of the book *You Can Always Sell More!*, Jim Pancero, a former top producer IBM and now a sales trainer and coach, was in town and she arranged a brief get-together. After our meeting, Jim left with my video demo, brochure, promotional pieces, and several autographed copies of my books. I left with his insightful suggestions on how I could improve my programs and materials. His mentoring has been invaluable, and it all started with a phone call to a friend who was kind enough to help out. Who could you ask to review your materials? Ask for their ruthless feedback. Their objective input could be just what you need to move your product samples up to the next level.

3. **Ask if you can use the contact's name to open other doors.** One of my favorite annual activities for several years has been hosting a celebrity golf tournament to raise money for breast cancer research. Several years ago, one of our committee members met Grammy award winner Amy Grant, who was in town representing Target Corporation and playing in a charity golf tournament. Our committee member asked Amy if she would return to Minnesota to be our lead entertainer for our golf event. Amy said she'd love to but instructed us from the get-go that she wouldn't be able to give us a firm decision until

approximately three weeks before our event in case she encountered any conflicts with her schedule. We knew it was an incredible risk, but we took it, crossed our fingers, and threw caution to the wind.

Three weeks before our event, she said she could come, and she did a marvelous job, thrilling us with her performance. We asked if she'd please come back the next year because she'd been so popular with our crowd. She told us she was already booked and would be unable to return. We asked if she could refer us to other celebrity golfers/entertainers, and she graciously complied. What a treat it was when Vince Gill and Hootie & the Blowfish took our calls on our first try . . . using Amy's name! Thanks, Amy—we hope to pay you back one of these days.

How do you use others' names to open your doors?

- Ask for permission. If possible, get a letter in writing granting you permission and fax or e-mail it to your prospect first.

- Frame your inquiry around why your friend or colleague granted permission for you to use his or her name. "I understand you're an avid tennis player. My client, Jim Irwin, suggested I give you a call because he has been using this new racket I represent."

- Create a connection: "Sue Stevens believes we have a lot in common, and I'm a big fan of Sue. I'm wondering if we can get together for a cup of coffee at your convenience."

4. **Serve as a resource to others.** One of my philosophies is that a shared gift of knowledge is a priceless gift to the spirit. Offer your expertise, services, knowledge, or your products *free* to the people you network with. You never know whom they might be networking with. Here's an example of how one free book turned into a very valuable account. This is a great example of connecting from the inside out.

I had contacted the vice president of sales for Coloplast Corporation with the hope of speaking to the company's national sales organization. Years went by, and although we had kept in touch, he hadn't yet asked me to keynote one of their conventions. I had originally sent him a copy of my first book, *Not Now . . . I'm Having a No Hair Day!* because their company makes breast prostheses for women who have undergone breast cancer surgery.

One day the webmaster for Coloplast, Bill Davis, who I had never spoken to, wandered into the vice president's office to discuss a new interactive website he was developing for the company. He happened to see my book sitting on the vice president's shelf and asked if he could borrow it. Bill was so moved by the content he contacted me to see if I would be interested in writing several articles for the company's website.

I happily agreed, and after submitting several articles, I suggested to Bill that I'd love to have the opportunity to speak to their national sales force. "You know, Bill, I could deliver an outstanding keynote address at next year's annual sales meeting. Your product line is right up my alley, and I've been getting tremendous feedback via e-mail from the articles you've been posting on your website. Would you please consider mentioning my name to the vice president of sales?"

Bill had been pleased with the response to my articles and cheerfully agreed to speak to the vice president. Lo and behold, soon after that I was scheduled as the keynote speaker for the company's national sales meeting in Salt Lake City. The moral of that story? It all counts. Connections are cumulative. If at first you don't succeed, you're about average. Persevere.

The story gets better. It just so happened that the European office had just hired a brand new international sales manager, and he'd been invited to attend this U.S. convention. I spent a lot of time preparing my presentation and included numerous mentions of the products and how the suggested techniques could be used in the company's workplace. A few months later, the international sales manager called to say he had been impressed and asked if I would like to come to Munich to address his international sales force. You can guess my answer.

At this meeting a representative was present from every European country. I attended all the breakfasts, lunches, and dinners; chatted with the representatives during the breaks; and stayed to watch the rest of the program. Within two months of that engagement, I was contacted by six other European sales managers with requests to speak in their countries. One sales manager even purchased the Hungarian rights to one of my books and had it published in Hungarian.

Let's backtrack this deal. By giving away just one free book and by being willing to write those articles, the business from this one customer expanded exponentially. I capitalized on creating connections from the inside out, kept my part of the bargain by delivering exemplary results, and used my existing contacts to keep the ball rolling.

5. **Put the experts on your mailing list.** Include the experts and connections you've made in your distribution lists for press releases, newsletters, new product introductions, and media appearances. You never know when something you are doing might catch someone's eye and bring you an unexpected phone call.

Cold Close

Let's address how you can create connections that drive your business from the outside in, working your way into a company or individual's inner circle. This is a challenging way of creating connections and is generally referred to as cold calling. But it's a mandatory component to keeping our avenues to new business open and can be successful by turning a cold call into a warm call.

Start by having a good script. If necessary, role-play with someone in your office or even with your significant other. Ask for feedback: "Did I sound pushy? Friendly? Knowledgeable? Did you want to learn more?" Gathering feedback is critical in putting your best foot forward.

I never like to come across as cold calling. I will do whatever it takes to find a connection with someone before I place the call. "I see you live in Edina. I raised my kids in Edina and now have my business based there. How long have you been living in Edina?" You've immediately engaged this person and created a bond between you, however distant.

Follow the lead of the person you're speaking with. If the person seems relaxed and easygoing, you can be more relaxed and easygoing, too. But if the person seems all business, then say something like, "I know your time is extremely valuable, so I'll get right to the point." Learning how and what people say can guide you in the direction of your pitch and presentation.

Turn a Cold Close Into a Warm Close

Kari Brannigan was a relatively new sales rep for a paper manufacturer, and her previous job experience had been in research for a brokerage firm. Kari decided that she would create Niche Notoriety by focusing on the brokerage industry, an enterprise that she correctly assumed would use a lot of paper. The problem she encountered is that no one would take her calls. Kari decided to grab the bull by the horns. She went to the nearest brokerage firm and asked the receptionist to direct her to a broker where she could open a new account.

Kari didn't have a lot of money to invest, but it was something she had intended to do for quite a while. Opening the new account gave her immediate access to someone within the organization who might have a need for her paper. She started dropping in on a regular basis, getting to know the secretary at the front desk and developing a friendship with her broker. Then, one day the office manager was in the lobby when Kari entered the building.

"Hi, Scott, I'm Kari Brannigan. You don't know me, but I am one of your accounts here. My broker, Laura, has done a terrific job with my account. By the way, I am a sales representative for a paper company, and I've noticed that your supplier is often not able to keep up with your demand. Do you think I might set up an appointment with you to show you what our company

71

has to offer? I'd like to drop off a case of our paper to acquaint you with our product line."

Bet you can imagine how that story turned out. Yes, Kari got the business. The office manager was so impressed with her resourcefulness that he decided she was the type of vendor he wanted to work with. Even if we have to start with a cold call, we can establish a commonality to get our foot in the door. Sending free samples or coupons or offering a free service is a terrific way to turn that cold call into a hot lead. Or you may want to try Kari's approach. To get an account, become an account.

Velocity

We've all experienced it sometime: "I never meet anyone"; "I can't seem to find new clients"; "I can't seem to find the right person for the job." You won't ever meet anyone, find new clients, or hire a new administrative assistant if you stay at home, hide in your cubicle, or fail to put out feelers.

Half of meeting and finding anyone is being out there. It's called velocity. The more you put yourself out there, the more likely it is that you will find who you're looking for.

Here's the Real Deal

- Don't fly blind. Don't sell blind. Research the possibilities.
- Create opportunities to meet the people you want to meet.
- Create the proper introductions. Be strategically savvy.
- Spend money to make money.
- Wait until the timing is right. Don't jump the gun.
- Find areas of commonality. Dig deep.

Chapter 7

Let's Partner a Deal

They might not need me, yet they might,
I'll let my head be just in sight;
A smile as small as mine might be
Precisely their necessity.

—Emily Dickinson

I 'm thinking about the Lone Ranger. Doesn't it seem significant that the person whose very name suggests solitude was never without his partner? Tonto did things the Lone Ranger couldn't and knew things his *kemo sabe* didn't. Together, each man was better than either could be alone.

So it is, I believe, in anything, including sales. Let's look at music, for example: Rodgers and Hammerstein, Burt Bacharach and Carole Bayer Sager, Elton John and Bernie Taupin—not to mention Lennon and McCartney or Elvis and Carl Perkins.

Everywhere we look, two heads can be better than one and can be the key to success. A rookie in a brokerage firm sets an appointment with a potentially large client and brings along his office manager to back him up. Two women join forces to start their own public relations firm. One has the media contacts, but the other has hundreds of connections. Together they make a great team and their company is successful. A coach guides the quarterback and their team to the Super Bowl. Tips and hints, advice and counsel, on and on. From these partnerships, each of us becomes better.

Sometimes forming partnerships can help us close our deals. Why? Because a second set of eyes and ears may hear or see things you might miss. A partner will often have different strengths that help offset your weaknesses. It may be as simple as the fact that you feel more confident when you have someone else to back you up. It seems best to start, as the poet Henry Reed put it, with "a naming of parts." What are the parts of a great partnership and how can they help you close more deals? I believe there are four parts. Let me elaborate.

First and foremost, there is trust, the glue of great relationships. We earn the trust of others by being consistent and by ensuring that we do what we say and say what we do. When others can predict what we will do, particularly from what we say, they feel comfortable. And that feeling is the heart of every great relationship and the heart of every sale. We want our customers to know with conviction that they can count on us, our product or service, and our company.

Can I Trust You?

There used to be a fabulous stationery store in Minneapolis where you could find unique cards, wrapping paper, gift items, and more. It was in an out-of-the-way strip mall, however, so it was a destination location—you made a decision that you were going to drive to that neighborhood to shop in that store.

The hours and days that the store was open were posted on their door, their website, and on their voice mail message. But the owner had other ideas or plans. Dozens of times when I'd arrive—often in the middle of the day—the store was closed. Notes would be left on the door: "Back in a half hour." The hours became so unreliable that I stopped shopping there. But guess what? So did everyone else. The store went out of business.

The second part of great partnerships is responsibility. But here it's worth noting the parts of that word: *response* and *ability*. We are able to respond to the requests of others. In today's climate, that also means we are able to respond quickly—ideally, in near real time.

I worked with an attorney on a variety of needs, both professionally and personally. Something critical came up that I needed an answer to as quickly as possible. I put several calls a day in to this attorney and left voice messages and sent e-mails. Days went by with no response. Finally, on the fifth day without hearing anything—from either him or someone in his office—I was reading the *USA Today* and opened the sports page. There on the front page was a quote from my attorney because he was representing a high-profile case involving athletes.

My conclusion? My business wasn't important to him or his firm. My solution? He isn't my attorney anymore. Ask yourself, "How quickly am I responding to the needs of my potential customers and my existing clients?" Be responsible and reliable.

The third part of a great partnership is sacrifice. When we sacrifice for others—for our clients, particularly—they see that we are there not just to perform and be paid but to give something extra of ourselves. I once heard a client describe the phenomenon of parachute speakers. When asked to elaborate, he said, "You know, the speaker who drops in, speaks, and pops back out—almost like a phantom." Your client doesn't simply want a stellar presentation; she wants to know that she matters, that her company matters, and that the speaker realizes the sacrifice she made. She took the risk of hiring you. You easily could have flopped, made an unfortunate remark, or demonstrated that you had no idea who your audience was. She made a sacrifice; you must make one, too.

The legendary first couple of the American theater, Hume Cronyn and Jessica Tandy, inspire my choice of the fourth key to partnerships. Their 52-year marriage inspired envy and awe in thousands who met them. Finally one day not long before Ms. Tandy died, someone thought to ask them how they had endured so long and with such apparent love. Mr. Cronyn answered immediately and with conviction. "It's simple, I think. We never said an impolite word to each other." The key to manners is mindfulness: being mindful of others. You can be confident, for example, that the person in the coffee shop speaking loudly enough into his cell phone that everyone within five tables can hear every word is not mindful of others. You can also be sure that he would not make a good partner. He thinks first of himself. A true partner thinks first of the partnership.

How do you decide if you need or want a partner? Ask yourself the following questions:

- Is there an area of my business that could benefit from the expertise of another, more knowledgeable person?
- Could bringing in a partner draw in more business by having a skill or talent that I don't have?
- Does this person have the same passions, beliefs, and aspirations I have to grow this business?
- Will having a partner make my life easier?
- Can I afford to have a partner?
- Am I willing to make sacrifices for this person?

If you can answer "yes" to these questions, you may be a person who could benefit from having a business partner. Let me give you some examples.

Get Close

In 1995, when I first started drawing cartoons of my cancer experience but had not yet found a publisher, I decided to hire a professional illustrator. I ran an ad, and hundreds of cartoonists and artists started contacting me by sending samples of their illustrations over the fax machine.

When Jack Lindstrom's illustrations came over the fax one morning, I just knew. Excitedly, I contacted him immediately, gave him two examples of my cartoons, and said, "Let's see what you can do with these." He captured the essence of me, my family, my dog, and most important, my sick sense of humor perfectly. He was hired on the spot.

Jack and I worked together for 17 years. I trusted him immediately—I knew he wasn't going to share my work with anyone who might steal my ideas. He was reliable, always showing up for our meetings and get-togethers early, prepared, and ready to work. He got me the cartoons I needed on a timely basis, often working under great pressure and severe deadlines. And he always put me ahead of himself. For all those years, Jack drew the cartoons for The Cancer Club newsletter . . . for free. He did it because we were partners.

Together Jack and I wrote five award-winning cartoon books on the subjects of finding humor in two very difficult topics: cancer and divorce. One morning last spring, Jack called me. His news? His beloved wife of 55 years, Jackie, had just had a double mastectomy the day before. His request was quite simple, really: "Chris, will you please do me a favor and write Jackie a note? I know it will mean the world to her."

I told him of course I would write her a note and asked him what else I could do. Assuring me that everything was under control for the time being, we said our good-byes and, as custom, I said, "Jack, I love you."

"Chris, I love you, too."

I immediately went into my office, found a beautiful card, and wrote Jackie a note. I walked it out to my mailbox and was pleased to see that the mail carrier hadn't come yet. "Great," I thought. "She'll get this note tomorrow." I also called Cookies by Design and ordered Jackie a cookie bouquet.

The next morning, my phone rang. Jack's name appeared on my iPhone. "Good morning, Jack," I started, thinking he's calling to thank me for the cookie bouquet.

"Christine, this isn't Jack. It's Jackie. We lost Jack last night."

"Where did he go?" I asked, not quite grasping the seriousness of what she was about to tell me.

"He died in his sleep last night."

Words could never begin to describe the loss I have experienced losing Jack. He was a friend, a colleague, a brother, a father, an illustrator, and my partner. I have officially retired from writing any additional cartoon books because he could never be replaced.

Jack was equally responsible for contributing to my success as an author and speaker because he made sacrifices for me. It's one of the true gifts that I've had in my life, and I was extremely blessed to know him.

Finally, it's hard to imagine a great partnership without passion. In a great partnership between you and your client, there is not merely a desire for a good outcome. There is a passion for a remarkable outcome. That outcome, in turn, is not to simply inform but to inspire. It is not to provide a great product or service but to have a great effect. In offering that suggestion, a remark by advertising legend David Ogilvy comes to mind. He told the story of audiences for the speeches of two famous Greeks. Of the first, audiences always remarked, "How well he speaks!" But of the second, they always responded, "Let us march on Sparta!" The first speaker impressed audiences; the second moved them. And it was his passion that inspired theirs.

As we all move ahead with our goals of inspiring clients to "march on Sparta," we all will do well to remember that even the Lone Ranger was not alone. At least two heads always are better than one. And partners—whether it is a mentor, supervisor, office manager, or friend—will help you get to Sparta, too, wherever your Sparta may be.

Multiple Close

If two heads are better than one, what would 10 heads look like?

All of us have role models—people we look up to, admire, respect, and want to emulate. Mine is Shirley Hutton Harris. She's the retired legendary top-producing independent national sales director emeritus for Mary Kay Cosmetics and author of *Pay Yourself What You're Worth*. Shirley has made a living from creating lifelong partnerships.

Shirley began her career at Mary Kay in 1973, making $12,000 that year, and learned immediately that she was in the business of building people, not selling cosmetics. As a direct marketing company, Mary Kay taught Shirley that she could be as successful as she wanted to be only by helping others succeed, too. She embraced the concept of partnerships and developed a strategy she calls "share the career." Shirley could not have achieved her success by going it alone.

I asked Shirley what the keys were to her success. In her business, as in all of ours, Shirley acknowledged that there were women of every possible socioeconomic level. She realized that she needed them to walk beside her as she led them. "Never be their superior," Shirley explained. "Always be their mentor. Never ask the independent beauty consultants to do anything you wouldn't do yourself. Don't stand on the stage in front of your partners like a band director, directing the band. Rather, become the Pied Piper. Lead them where you are going."

Think about the business of selling and the partnerships that we build in our businesses. Vendors, sponsors, volunteers, committee members, project managers, the receptionist . . . How often are we called upon by people beginning their sales careers to help them get started, review their fledgling marketing materials, or point them in the right direction? If we take Shirley's approach, to "share our careers," we take the time, *make* the time, to bring as many partners into our lives as possible.

There are many ways for you to keep your partnerships strong, such as:

- Ensuring that you are all being treated fairly and equally
- Allowing each other space, downtime, or just a break when you need it
- Putting their needs above yours
- Asking, "How can I help?"
- Treating each other with respect and honesty
- Covering for each other
- Always having each other's back

The benefits of having strong partnerships are enormous: They alleviate your workload; bring fresh and new ideas into your company or organization; take pressure off you to be "all things to all people"; and add depth and growth to your business. But one thing to consider is that we are all different: One partner may want to be front and center, the eyes and ears of the company—managing media requests, appearing at banquets and fund-raisers, or speaking at company meetings and functions. The other partner may wish to lie in the weeds, so to speak—keeping a lower profile, staying out of the public eye, and managing the back office instead. Just like in a marriage, there is give and take. Building partnerships takes time, dedication, and a sincere desire to do business with another person. Some partnerships are quite public and both parties appear one and the same. In other partnerships, your clients and prospects may never even know you have a partner; the interactions only involve one of you or the other. In Chapter 14, we'll discuss how to create loyals for life (long-term customers who keep coming back year after year). The same characteristics that apply to customer loyalty are even more important when dealing with partners. We can always get another client, but we may never get another partner.

Partnerships in Your Profession

So how can you create partnerships in your profession? Partner with the competition. I stopped in my neighborhood hardware store the other day looking for a very rare battery. When the clerk found they didn't stock it, she pulled out the business card of another hardware store in a neighboring community and said, "Give them a call. I'm confident they'll carry the battery you're looking for." I called them and they did carry it. But that onetime purchase didn't cause me to change suppliers. Now I have even more confidence and trust in my store because they went out on a limb for me. My business mattered to them, and they made a sacrifice.

Carefully choose other sales experts who offer a similar, if not identical, product or service and offer a comparable fee. If a client calls you to place an order and you can't fill it for any reason, have a list of these contacts that you can willingly refer. You may wish to set up a small referral fee or percentage for your efforts. Whatever you do, creating partnerships with competitors is a goodwill gesture that your clients will never forget.

When prospects call who can't accommodate your going rate or price, refer them to companies with similar products but smaller requirements. If they can't afford you, they aren't the right client for you anyway. I always say, "What goes around comes around." If your competitors have a lower-quality product or service, eventually the client you referred will probably find their way back to you. Quality always trumps price. But they will always remember that you were willing to give up their business to help them out.

The second key to Shirley's success and her company's, by and large, is public praise and recognition. We all recognize the most visible sign of success at Mary Kay: the pink Cadillac. But although rewards come in the way of furs, diamonds, trips, and prizes, Shirley believes public acknowledgment was the most significant motivator. Posting "Winner of the Week" on her website or awarding that pole position parking to the "Woman of the Month" keeps her partners motivated and energized.

Think about your base of customers and ask, "When is the last time I gave recognition to my clients, my partners?" Create a "Client of the Month" and "Client of the Year" contest based on a set of measurable and nonmeasurable criteria. Determine who gave you the most business, was easiest to work with, has hired you back year after year, and referred additional business. Then reward your clients publicly by giving them a small trophy or certificate, taking them to dinner, and posting the announcement on your website or Facebook or Twitter account or in your e-zine or newsletter. You'll be amazed at how quickly that client refers you more business!

There were 40,000 independent beauty consultants at Mary Kay when Shirley started in 1973. When she retired in 1995, she had recruited 20,000 consultants, in all 50 states plus Canada and Mexico, on her own. In 21 years, Shirley earned more than $7 million and retired to the tune of $8 million to be paid over a 15-year period. Not bad for a few years of hard work, dedication, and strong partnerships.

As you think about growing your business, remember that we're in the business of building people, too: Our clients, our employees, our colleagues, and our communities can and will lead us to our ultimate success. As Shirley said to me in her closing comments, "Two heads are better than one. But 10 heads are better than two."

Other successful people know and understand this philosophy, too.

Golf is a very solitary sport. Sure, you can play in a foursome or partner in a match. Perhaps a caddy is following you (hopefully down the fairway) for 18 holes. But when it's all said and done, golfers play against themselves and the course alone. Or so it only seems.

Renowned golf architect Bill Coore created one of the most successful partnerships in golf, pairing with former Masters Champion Ben Crenshaw to design acclaimed courses including Sand Hills, Talking Stick, and Bandon Preserve in Oregon. Speaking of partnerships, Bill is married to Sue Hershkowitz-Coore, CSP, a highly accomplished author and professional speaker.

I asked Bill, "What experience in business taught you the most?" He said that while working with the legendary architect Pete Dye in the early 1970s, Bill asked Pete for career advice, and that advice changed Bill's perspective forever: "Get to know the bulldozer drivers."

Bill believes you can be the world's most visionary architect, full of magical ideas, but your ideas will still fail without the bulldozer drivers—the partners who transform your ideas into magic and contribute magic of their own.

Selling resembles golf. We, too, may have support staff, accountants, printers, or coaches who help us. But when we step up to the board table, it's really up to us to deliver our best performance. How can we ensure that we do this every time?

Get to know the people who drive *our* bulldozers.

Who are those people? Start by arriving at your sales destination an hour or two earlier than scheduled. Eat lunch in the cafeteria or ask if you can tour the facility. Meet as many members/employees/volunteers as possible. Establishing a partnership with your customer helps ensure that they enjoy your presentation, invite you to return, and refer you to others.

Find the people who will be setting up your meeting room, running your audiovisual equipment, turning down the lights, and closing and opening the doors. Their cooperation and willingness to partner with you can be the difference between a good performance and a great one—or between a good one and a disaster.

Bill Coore believes these principles of partnership are the key to his success. Bill believes that he and Ben must establish the framework of their design and concept and keep the widest possible focus. During the process that follows, they refine their focus without ever limiting the ideas or suggestions of others—the people driving the bulldozers. By allowing people to do what they know how to do best, the end result is the betterment of the whole group and the entire project.

Think about the time you walked into a meeting room, not long before your starting time, and found the arrangement of the tables and chairs not to your liking. In a panic, you may have chastised the maintenance workers, who tried in vain to assure you that the arrangement was the optimum for acoustics, accessibility, sight lines, and audiovisual equipment. They probably had very good reasons for what they had done; after all, they—like you—probably have been doing what they were doing for a long time. At moments like these, remember what Pete told Bill: *Listen to the guys on the bulldozers.*

Finally, I asked Bill what other significant partnerships played a role in his success. He immediately responded, "My partnership with my wife, Sue." He explained that Sue always listens to his ideas, offers her encouragement, and makes suggestions wherever she feels her own expertise could help. "I could *never* have achieved my success without her."

So, in selling as in golf, are we ever really alone? No. I think not. We all owe a tremendous amount of our success to the people who drive our bulldozers. Get to know *your* drivers. Thank them for their contributions. Then go out and create a masterpiece based on partnerships. They will make you better; you can make them better; and the result will be not just an outstanding pitch but a deeply gratifying experience for everyone.

So are there any additional ways you can form strategic partnerships? You wouldn't have ventured into your field if you didn't have something powerful to pitch. My guess is that you've become an expert in your industry, or you would have gone back to job searching long ago. So do you want to spend your valuable time, money, and efforts marketing and selling one product here and another there? Or do you want to propel your expertise into a seven-figure income by securing a single client?

How? Become a celebrity or corporate spokesperson.

Become a Celebrity or Corporate Spokesperson

What? "I'm not famous," you're thinking. I didn't think I was either until I was recently hired to star in a Hollywood-made documentary. When the Hollywood producers did a Google search for "cancer survivors," my name kept popping to the top of their list. When they contacted me to discuss starring in their documentary, I was able to immediately send over my marketing kit, including accomplishments, articles, references, and links to hundreds of connections that could help them make the documentary a success. This all happened as a result of spending money to make money: I had invested in myself—in my website, marketing materials, and presence—to put myself in the path of luck. Pay more now; reap more later.

Still don't think you'll be discovered?

Make a Pitch to Serve in Media Campaigns

Take your knowledge to corporations or organizations that sell products or services that could benefit from your expertise. Make a pitch to serve as a spokesperson on their behalf. Design a professional proposal that outlines why you are a strong candidate; what you believe you can do for their product, service, or sales force; how you would implement your position; and what the expected return on investment would be for each organization. As part of your proposal, offer to participate in all media campaigns on the corporation's or organization's behalf.

I served in this capacity for three years for Health East Care Systems, a full-service, U.S.-based health care system. They were opening a new breast cancer center and wanted some higher visibility. Besides the seven-figure fees that can be negotiated for serving in such a capacity (i.e., Ashton Kutcher and Nikon; Michael Phelps and Subway; Phil Mickelson and Rolex), this client alone generated dozens of speaking engagements per year for me, made significant product purchases, and generated more than 300 media appearances for me on their behalf.

Develop a celebrity image that will elevate you above your peers. If you do your research and think creatively, you could find yourself promoting somebody's product and have a great time doing it, too.

How to start? Make a list of companies or organizations whose products or services might benefit from your expertise. Greg Godek, who speaks about romance and relationships and wrote *1001 Ways to Be Romantic,* could be perfect for many sponsors: Champagne distributors, flower vendors, perfume manufacturers, and greeting card companies are among the obvious choices.

Contact the vice president of marketing for these companies and open with the following statement: "I've been following your company and have some products and services that may help you sell more of yours." Ask the following questions:

- Does your company have or has it ever had a corporate spokesperson?
- Can I send you a proposal outlining how I can benefit your company?
- Can you make a list of everything you might do on the company's behalf? Some examples include:
  - Attending trade shows, community-related functions, and conferences to help promote a new product or service

- Providing internal seminars to the sales force, clients, or vendors on your subject, product, or service

- Acting as a liaison with the media to enhance the company's image

- Developing educational materials such as booklets, newsletters, or pamphlets for the company's employees, customers, or vendors

- Functioning as a valued authority for customers by writing an online column for the company's website or blog

- Serving as an advocate of the public by attending internal meetings or serving on a committee to bring an "outsider's perspective" to the way that the company does business

- Planning a special event such as a golf tournament, fashion show, or fund-raiser to increase awareness of a specific product or service.

The key is to position yourself as a partner who can help bring that company added value and exposure to *its* product, service, or cause.

How else can you help? A corporate spokesperson can find new customers the company has not had access to in the past. Offer to secure sales presentations on your subject matter on their behalf, with the sponsor paying you a fee and expenses. You may want to offer a volume discount. You, in turn, put up their point-of-purchase materials on-site, hang a banner with the corporate logo, and ensure that the company is acknowledged as your sponsor in all written materials, including press releases, program materials, proposals, and signs or posters.

Whether you work in health care, technology, real estate, or banking, there are potential sponsors. To prove this, look at the program for the next industry conference you attend. What do you see? Dozens of companies and individuals who teamed up to make that conference happen. Then go out there and create a uniquely powerful partnership—the partnership between companies and their spokespersons.

If a related corporation or organization backs away from having you as a spokesperson, present Plan B, which is to partner with that corporation for maximum exposure. By obtaining corporate sponsorship for your company, you in turn will provide the organization with deeper penetration and accessibility to potential clients it could not obtain without utilizing your services.

What exactly is corporate sponsorship? It's when two companies partner together—yours and another company—to gain wider distribution of products or services. You both benefit from such a relationship. Although you may not be an official spokesperson for this company, gaining corporate sponsorship can help you cover your costs of doing business, elevate your presence above its current level, and help you close more deals.

Jaime Hansen, a financial advisor for Morgan Stanley, had heard about my first Divorcing Divas conferences and asked me to meet her for a cup of coffee. Right away I informed Jaime that I was not personally looking for a new financial advisor and we had already secured our presenting sponsor for the next conference—a sponsorship that included exclusivity in that category (financial services).

But Jaime wasn't one to take the first "no" as the final "no." At our next conference, she attended and brought her sister. At the following conference, she purchased a full table for 10. Finally, a door opened: the presenting sponsorship became available. Because Jaime had been in constant touch with me, she was the first one I thought of and I gave her a call. "We're all in!" she said.

But Jaime didn't stop there. She continued to Perk-O-Late our relationship by hosting special events and inviting me to bring guests. She hired my son Brooks as an intern; this position resulted in him getting a full-time job offer as a financial advisor. She took me out on her boat, hosted a wine tasting for all our other sponsors, and helped me "man" a booth at a trade show. The icing on the cake for Jaime? Because she had gone so above and beyond and had clearly demonstrated her long-term commitment to being a strategic partner with me, I turned my assets over to her for management and have been referring her ever since.

Corporate sponsorships are a way for both of you to achieve what it is you're striving for, while at the same time providing each other new outlets for business. Seek out companies that you think you could promote and partner with. It's one of the ways to generate that seven-figure income!

Are you creating partnerships that will last for years and years? Doing what we say we will do and exceeding our clients' expectations time and time again will help us create powerful partnerships.

Here's the Real Deal

- Partners have strengths to offset your weaknesses.
- Trust is the glue of great relationships.
- Be responsible and reliable.
- A true partner thinks of the partnership.
- Building partnerships takes time, dedication, and a sincere desire to do business with another person.
- Become a celebrity or corporate spokesperson.
- Build strategic corporate sponsorships.

Let's Present the Deal

Before I can sell John Jones
What John Jones buys,
I must see the world
Through John Jones's eyes.

—**Anonymous**

Chapter 8

Let's Pitch a Deal

Your deal is now perfectly packaged; you've established that it fills a void in the marketplace and you've created solid connections. What's next? It's time to pitch your deal. Have you ever gone to market with what you thought was a well-prepared sales call, but you didn't close the deal? Could it have been the way you pitched the deal that made them walk away?

In this chapter, we'll cover how to dot all your i's and cross all your t's so the client concludes your deal is the best one. Often pitches fail because of fear. If you can prepare yourself by planning for success, you will succeed.

> *There is nothing final about a mistake, except its being taken as final . . .*
>
> —Phyllis Bottome

You've all heard the expression, "You never get a second chance to make a first impression." Because you only get one shot at your first pitch, it's critical that you anticipate everything that can go wrong. It's human nature to think of all the things that can go right: "I'll get this sale and then I'll make quota. My commission check will allow me to buy that new dress I've been eyeballing. Maybe now I'll get that promotion I've wanted." But don't let the buggy get before the horse. Here's an example of a perfect pitch that went terribly wrong.

Case Closed

The Cancer Club had been in business for several years before we developed enough products to have a full line to offer retailers, wholesalers, and so on.

One of the primary markets where I thought we could have a considerable impact was with the pharmaceutical industry. I mentioned in a previous chapter that the pharmaceutical company Schering Oncology Biotech purchased an exercise video for women recovering from breast cancer surgery to use as a product premium to introduce a new drug they were bringing to market.

This was a splendid win-win-win. I certainly benefited because Schering bought 65,000 copies of my video, a significant purchase for The Cancer Club. Schering was benefiting from the purchase by using the video (premium) to open doors to the offices of the doctors and nurses they wanted to call on to sell their new prescription medication. And breast cancer patients everywhere were benefiting from receiving the video *free* from the oncology offices and clinics that had been contacted by the Schering sales reps.

Wanting to expand this huge potential premium market, I networked like crazy to get in touch with the decision makers at another pharmaceutical giant, Bristol-Myers Squibb. Lance Armstrong was serving as their spokesperson, and I had presented several programs throughout the United States that had been sponsored by Bristol. I thought, "If I could just get an opportunity to show the senior executives my products, perhaps I could represent them in some way, too."

I started by calling my own oncology clinic and getting the name of the local Bristol rep who called on that office. After securing the name, I made my first contact. "Gail, my name is Christine Clifford, and I am a cancer survivor who used one of your drugs during my treatment process. I am now CEO of a company called The Cancer Club, which markets humorous and helpful products for people with cancer. I have several items that we have created that I feel may be of interest to you and Bristol for possible use as product premiums to complement your line. Would this be of interest to you?" Gail told me that as a local sales representative, she was not in a position to make such decisions. However, she would get in touch with her district manager, Ken, and would get back to me. Several weeks later, Gail called me back with good news.

Ken had supplied her with the name and telephone number of the woman at corporate headquarters who was exactly the person I needed to reach.

I immediately placed a call to the woman who was responsible for strategic alliances and patient support. "Rebecca, my name is Christine Clifford, and I've been given your name from Ken, the district manager for the Midwest, who believes that the work I am doing may be of interest to you and Bristol-Myers Squibb. I have worked with Bristol in several capacities, both on the consumer products side of your business when I worked for a marketing company and currently as a speaker at events being sponsored by Bristol on behalf of their oncology products. I am president of a company called The Cancer Club and have developed several products that I think may be of interest to you either as product premiums or for patient education. What questions can I answer that can help you determine whether we have a good fit?"

Rebecca expressed interest and said that her company was always looking for new items that could be used for just such a thing. She asked for some product samples.

Wanting to capitalize on this ripe opportunity, I put together one of my fully loaded marketing kits. I autographed books, stuck articles in the packet about the work I had already done in her industry, and included several letters of recommendation from Bristol reps who had utilized my speaking services.

I waited a week to make sure the products had arrived and then followed up. "Christine, you look like you have developed quite an interesting array of products," Rebecca replied. "I would like to schedule some time on your calendar when you could come to our offices and meet with our entire marketing department."

The entire marketing department? Yippee! We scheduled a date, and I put the wheels in motion. I drafted a professional proposal of exactly what I believed I could do for their company and their patients. I had custom labels made for our audiocassettes, CDs, and videos with their logo on them. I packed samples to give away to all the people who would be attending the meeting and flew off to Princeton, New Jersey. Every *i* had been dotted, and every *t* had been crossed.

Except for one . . . I broke one of my very own rules: It takes money to make money. In my effort to save a little money (after all, I was paying for my airfare, hotel, meals, etc.), I decided when I arrived I would rent a car and drive to their offices. I had been there several times in the past when I had been calling on their consumer packaged goods group, and I thought I knew the way. When I landed on the morning of our appointment (a noon luncheon with 11 individuals), I immediately went to the phone and called Rebecca to let her know I had landed. It was only 10:00 AM, and I had plenty of time, she assured me. Only I never anticipated the problems that were about to begin . . .

First, the suitcases I had packed with samples were so heavy that I could barely lift them off the luggage rack. Second, because of the size of the suitcases, I had to take an elevator to get up to the second floor of the airport instead of the escalator to take a tram to the car rental facility. There was only one elevator on the lower level, and it was malfunctioning. I ended up schlepping the heavy bags to the second floor by stairs, and then it took another 15 minutes to catch the tram to take me to my rental car. Forty-five minutes to spare . . . I finally got out of the airport and hit the freeways of New Jersey, only to travel for 15 minutes . . . in the wrong direction! Remember now: This was in the days before GPS! Thirty minutes and counting . . .

Once I finally got to the Bristol compound, already flustered and perspiring, I pulled out the directions that Rebecca had sent to me and tried to decipher which of the four large buildings I was facing was *her* building. It didn't say on the map. I unloaded my two huge suitcases, lugged them all the way into the lobby of Building 1, and asked for Rebecca. "I'm sorry, but she isn't in this building. I believe you want Building 2."

I went back to my car, drove to the next building, and went through the same drill. I called Rebecca to let her know what was happening only to receive her voice mail. I left a message and then another as I continued to search in vain for her office. Finally, the receptionist in Building 4 contacted her and handed me the phone, "Christine, this is Rebecca. I'm sorry I didn't receive your phone messages, but we were all gathered in the conference room waiting for your arrival. When you didn't show, we ate our lunches, and when you still weren't here by 1:15 PM, everyone had to leave for other meetings. I'm sorry, but we'll just have to make it another day."

I had missed my golden opportunity. If I had played devil's advocate and tried to anticipate all the things that *might* have gone wrong, I would have built in a bigger time cushion for Murphy's Law. If I had only had the foresight to hire a driver, a time-saving procedure I had done many times in the past when conducting business in strange cities, then he could have helped me with my luggage, and we would have been out to the compound with plenty of time to spare to find the right building. But I didn't think of every eventuality and paid a painful price.

The point for now is that if you want to close a deal, it's important to think in advance about anything that *could* go wrong so that you can either eliminate it or prepare for it and handle it with poise if it materializes. I also suggest you play what I call angel's advocate. As you can imagine, this is the opposite of devil's advocate. Instead of anticipating everything that can go wrong, anticipate everything that can go right. By doing so, you can visualize positive outcomes, which can increase their likelihood of happening. This isn't putting the cart before the horse, by the way. It's more about putting positive energy into yourself and the universe.

Super Close

If you drive into a strip mall in Golden Valley, Minnesota, your wildest imagination could never prepare you for what's behind the door of a nondescript office called Schussler Creative. But once you step over the threshold, you are carried into the magical world of a man named Steven Schussler.

Steven went on to create some of the world's most recognized themed restaurants, including Rainforest Café, T-REX, and Yak & Yeti Restaurant featured in Walt Disney World Orlando. But long before he achieved his enormous success, he nearly killed himself trying.

Steve tells the story in his best-selling book, *It's a Jungle in There: Inspiring Lessons, Hard-Won Insights, and Other Acts of Entrepreneurial Daring,* much better than I can, but here's the gist:

At the age of 18, Steve discovered he could make money selling airtime for radio and television stations. After interviewing for five months, he kept running into the same story: "You're the next guy we're going to hire." Too young and with no sales experience, he was hitting a roadblock every time.

Steve didn't get where he is today by thinking small. He purchased a wooden barrel, large enough to fit in; bought himself a Superman costume; and stopped by the apartment of two friends, who happened to be Miami-Dade police officers. Paying them each $100 to deliver him to one of the top radio stations, Steve played angel's advocate and packed a salami sandwich, a pickle, and a can of Diet Coke for his journey.

The next morning, the police officers showed up in full uniform, stuffed Steve and his lunch in the barrel, and nailed it shut. Then they hoisted him into their police van for the trip across town to the station.

It only took 5 minutes before Steve realized he'd made two enormous errors: One, he hadn't drilled holes in the barrel to allow oxygen in. Two, he had forgotten how hot Miami could be when you're stuffed in a barrel in 100° heat!

Today it's a sidesplitting experience to hear Steve share the rest of the story. Gasping for air and sweating like a pig, he prayed that he wouldn't die in a Superman costume stuffed in a barrel with a spoiled salami sandwich and a Diet Coke that had exploded because of the heat.

By the time they reached the station, Steve had to wait even longer because the station manager he was delivering himself to was at a board meeting. The receptionist called the manager to come investigate the barrel that had just been delivered, and he arrived with his entire board. Prying open the barrel, Steve flew out like a jack-in-the-box, gasping for air and wiping soda and salami from his face. He smiled at everyone and said,

"Hello, everybody, my name is Steve Schussler. I'm your new Super Salesman!"

One of the oldest board members turned to Steve and said, "Son, you are the sickest person we've ever met. You're hired!"

Fortunately for Steve, and for all of us who have enjoyed the restaurants he's created, Steve survived. But this story illustrates how careful we need to be when planning our pitch. The smallest details can be a matter of life and . . . well, death.

Before you make your pitch, write down all the things—every tiny step—on your angel's advocate list that you'd love to have happen from logistics, to handing out product samples, to how many copies/samples/products you will need, to potential questions that may arise, to closing the deal. Then make a devil's advocate list and address what could potentially go wrong with each of these points or steps. That way, at least you have thought about what could happen if something goes wrong or doesn't go the way you are hoping or expecting it to go.

Prior to making your pitch, try on your close: Imagine how your potential customer will feel, taste, and experience your product, service, or cause. Visualize what attracted you to your company, product, or service, and try to remember how you felt the first time you saw your product or heard about your powerful cause. You want to make your customer experience this, too.

Locking the Deal

By 1986, the Super Bowl had already become the biggest television event in America.

Dan Witkowski's small company MagiCom consisted of a part-time administrative assistant and himself when he approached the National Football League (NFL) with a strategy to increase its viewership. Prepared that his phone call would not make it past the receptionist at the, he found himself on the line with Jim Steeg, the NFL Director of Special Events, who was largely responsible for the institution that the Super Bowl had become. Steeg listened politely to Dan's pitch, and agreed to a follow-up face-to-face meeting in New York.

Dan's strategy was to use the half-time show as a vehicle to attract the non-football fans as well as football loyalists to tune into a new style of interactive half-time show where viewers at home could participate and interact with their television sets. Steeg explained that he and the NFL executives were willing to see Dan's presentation; however, he made it clear that Dan was in competition with the big boys: The Walt Disney Company, Warner Bros., Paramount Pictures, Radio City Music Hall, etc.

Dan versus Goliath

While it was clear that Dan's competition was formidable, he speculated that his competitors would focus on presenting options for great entertainment, but they might overlook the needs of the NFL to create something that would result in a seismic change in half-time shows. Dan's emphasis was on a strategy for increasing the size of the television viewing audience, which was directly transferable to added income versus simply producing a great show.

Even with a strong strategy in his pocket, he was a virtual unknown. So, to make up for his lack of awareness, Dan played both devil's advocate and angel's advocate, and went overboard on his research and preparation.

He studied every major football stadium in the country, and secured actual blueprints for most of them. (All public and most private buildings have to submit blueprints to the local county for permit approval; thus, these documents are matters of public record.)

Dan analyzed conditions in the cities most likely to host games: wind velocity, barometric pressure, possible sites for rehearsal, emergency preparations, access to local hospitals, security, talent base, everything. His "bible" of facts looked like he was going to war, and he knew that was the type of prep work that the big boys were not likely to do in advance.

Visualize the Experience

After his homework on the facilities and operations, Dan set to work on the fun part: depicting the show he was proposing for the NFL. It was a collage of striking colorful graphics and computer animation (and back in 1986, that was an industry in its infancy). Each illustration, storyboard, and picture was more impressive than the next. In short, it was the most detailed and comprehensive presentation his company had ever assembled. He was ready to wow them, and then, near disaster struck: submission of the show concept in writing in advance!

Several weeks before the presentation in New York, Dan received a letter from the NFL requesting that he submit a written summary of the show concept in advance of the live presentation. The NFL wanted to preview the concepts rather than have their entire top executives sit through 10 long presentations.

Disaster!

Trying to describe the spectacle, which was dependent on lavish costumes, scenery, dance, and special effects, would have been like handing someone who does not read music the score for Gershwin's *Rhapsody in Blue* and saying "What do you think?"

It was all about the visual experience timed with the music, the motion, and the color. Words could describe the action, but doing justice to the spirit of the show was another matter entirely.

Dan had no choice but to comply with the wishes and requirements of the NFL, yet how could he maintain the important element of surprise that is inherent in a magic show? This would be the largest magic and illusion show in history, and magic depends on the element of surprise in order to be successful.

Inspiration—and Bending the Rules

A call to the NFL confirmed that there would be no exceptions to this rule, so Dan complied by assembling a book to describe his show. A separate book was prepared for each NFL executive with the show title and the executive's name stamped on the leather cover in silver.

As he prepared to pack each book in a FedEx overnight box, inspiration struck. He reread the letter, and it was clear that he needed to submit this outline. But what it did *not* say was that the NFL did not have to READ the show descriptions.

Quickly he and his assistant returned to the printer that helped them prepare the books with a request that they punch a hole through each book. After gathering the 12 presentation books, he went to a locksmith to purchase 12 matching brass-and-chrome locks to seal the books shut.

On top of each book was a note indicating how he had complied with the rules of the NFL; however, he felt that the element of surprise was so important to his plans for the show, the keys to the books would be distributed at the end of his live presentation in New York.

It was a gutsy move, and one that could have easily backfired. But the next day, Dan received a call from Jim Steeg, who said Dan's little diversion created a great deal of talk in the NFL's executive suites.

Suddenly, for better or worse, the name MagicCom, which was completely unknown to the NFL's executive team, became the source of office buzz. So much so that two weeks later, when Dan went before the NFL to make his live presentation, 11 out of 12 of the NFL's executive team were in attendance, including Football Commissioner Pete Rozelle, the man who literally created the Super Bowl.

Commissioner Rozelle was the man who made the NFL the powerhouse it is today. He was a public relations man who understood that if you had a good story to tell, people would flock to listen.

He did not let Dan off easily, at least at first. "Mr. Witkowski, before you begin, could you tell us why you did not follow the League rules regarding submission of your show concept?"

"Mr. Commissioner, in fact we did comply, yet we took advantage of the loophole that did not clarify [that] our submission needed to be in a form that was easily accessible."

Silence.

Then the commissioner's eyebrows raised, and a sheepish grin appeared on his face. "I'm not sure if I should watch your half-time presentation, or offer you a job in the legal department," he laughed. His chuckles were joined by the rest of the executives in the room, and from that point on, Dan's presentation could not have gone any smoother.

At the end of the presentation, true to Dan's word, every executive in attendance received a key to unlock his or her presentation book.

There was one executive, Val Pinchbeck, the head of NFL network relations, who did not attend. The next day, Pinchbeck asked Rozelle for the key to his book, and Rozelle chided him by saying, "You read the note: attend the meeting and you will get the key. Sorry, Val."

Jim Steeg later told Dan that his was the only presentation that Pete Rozelle attended that year.

The "Key" to Closing the Deal

In this example, the "key" to closing the deal between the National Football League and MagiCom was literally a key.

The "key" became the device that they remembered MagiCom for, yet the advance preparation and detail, as well as having a strong strategic concept, made Dan's offer stand out.

The result of all of this was well worth the effort.

- The NFL awarded Dan two contracts: one to create a new spectacle concept for the Super Bowl XXII Opening Ceremonies as well as the half-time show for Super Bowl XXIII the following year.

- Since Dan's strategy was based on making the half-time show interactive with television viewers, he premiered a new 3-D technology that became the first telecast of a network television program in 3-D surround sound in history to an audience of one billion people worldwide.

- A sponsor, Diet Coke, also produced a commercial in 3-D that aired immediately after the half-time show.

- The Super Bowl XXIII game was broadcast for the first time in China that year, and had a worldwide viewing audience of over one billion people, making it the most watched magic event in history.

- Worldwide media attention generated over $60,000,000 in international publicity for Diet Coke and the show.

- The show featured over 2,000 performers, a card trick involving 75,000 people in the stadium, and 102 new custom-made chrome and white Harley-Davidson motorcycles in the finale.

- All together, the resulting media exposure for MagicCom resulted in approximately $132,000,000 in worldwide media awareness.

How can you transfer these emotions that you once—or perhaps still—feel when you talk about what it is you are selling? Do it with unbridled enthusiasm. Get your potential customers so pumped up about what you are selling or servicing that they can't help but want to get involved with you and your company.

Become Your Own Barnum & Bailey

My manuscript *Cancer Has Its Privileges* had been finished and Perigee, a division of Penguin Putnam, had purchased the rights to publish the book. I had obtained my Foreword from Dr. Buck and my Introduction from Arnold Palmer. Now it was time to publish the book. My editor called with the bad news: "Christine, we don't want to call the book *Cancer Has Its Privileges*. We want to call it *The Cancer Club*.

"The Cancer Club?!" I thought with disdain. This will *never* work. Visualize my appearance on *The Today Show* or *CNN* and they introduce me, "Ladies and gentlemen, today we have author Christine Clifford, president and CEO of The Cancer Club, with her new book, *The Cancer Club . . .* " Well, this simply would not work.

I went to business writing down all the reasons that the book should be called *Cancer Has Its Privileges* and the reasons why it should never be called *The Cancer Club.* First, the title was the essence of what I was writing about: all the gifts that had come to me as a result of being diagnosed with cancer. To the contrary, I argued, no pharmaceutical company would even dream of purchasing the rights to the book to use as a product premium if they thought they were promoting a company (The Cancer Club), rather than just a book. And besides, I owned the trademark and copyright to the words, so I simply would not grant permission.

Then I asked to speak to the publisher himself. They granted me the appointment. I went right to work, acting as my own Barnum & Bailey promoting and talking about what worked and what didn't. When we ended the call, the publisher said, "You're right, Christine. You win."

The very next day, FedEx rang my doorbell. I don't know about you, but to me, FedEx is like Santa in shorts. I ripped open the envelope and found four glossy prototypes of the book's cover with the title *Cancer Has Its Privileges* in bold blue letters. "Introduction by Arnold Palmer" was printed below my name, and "Foreword by Clarence H. Brown III, M.D." was below that.

The publisher had sent me the covers to proofread, and when I was done proofing, my mind started spinning with ideas. Who could I send these four beautifully laminated covers to help me publicize my book? Oprah Winfrey? Barbara Walters? Katie Couric?

I stuck them in my briefcase, and the very next day I had my yearly exam with my oncologist. As I waited for my name to be called, I decided to stop in and see the patient representative, Margie Sborov, who had been so kind to me when I was going through my treatments. Margie and I had worked on a few programs together, and she had made arrangements for me to speak to the patients on several occasions. She had also purchased numerous copies of my first two books and had given them away to patients and their families.

When I walked in to Margie's office, she greeted me warmly. With unbridled enthusiasm, I pulled out my four invaluable book covers and showed her my newest achievement. I looked up and realized that Margie was crying. She was so moved and touched by what I had done (remember: she had seen me only years before: bald, sick, and battling cancer) that she was speechless. I decided then and there that I was going to give Margie one of the four precious book covers.

I autographed it and wrote, "Margie, this is for all the wonderful things you have done for me over the years." She accepted it gratefully and said she was going to get it framed.

As I stood up to leave, I saw some pens on her desk from a pharmaceutical company. I said, "Margie, I know you have a lot of pharmaceutical reps who come to call on you and the clinic. If you should get the opportunity, would you please show them this book cover and see if one of them might have an interest in helping distribute it for us?"

Only one day had passed when a sales rep from Aventis Pharmaceuticals walked into Margie's office. Still sitting on her desk was the autographed copy of the book cover. Margie told the rep about me, my previous work, and this book. That afternoon, I got a call from the Aventis rep. "Christine, with your permission, I'd like to share the information about your new book with my district manager in Chicago."

Days later when the district manager contacted me, he said, "Christine, our entire sales force and the decision makers about product premiums will all be meeting in San Antonio, Texas, next week. Do you think you can join us for a meeting?"

This time, I wanted to make no mistakes, so I played angel's advocate. I wrote down all the questions I thought they might have about me, the book, my company, and anything else I thought could arise. I solicited the help of my publisher ahead of time so I had pricing in case they wanted to make a bulk purchase. I wasn't about to lose this sale by not being prepared. If I had said to them, "Oh, let me get in touch with my publisher to see what this might cost," we would lose momentum; they may change their minds; or the competition might come to them with a better offer.

On the day of my meeting, the deal was closed. Aventis purchased 70,000 copies of my book before it even hit the bookstores and gave them away to cancer patients and oncology clinics across the nation.

To what do I credit making this sale? Playing angel's advocate and mapping out all the good things that I thought would come out of this transaction helped me prepare, pitch, and close. Asking for help from Margie, or partnering as we discussed in Chapter 7, was invaluable. I couldn't have done it without her. And pitching my product with unbridled enthusiasm— acting as my own Barnum & Bailey—drew in all those I came in contact with. They couldn't help but want to do business with me.

These "It's so simple" (ISS) steps can take away the fear of pitching; give you confidence to present your pitch in the best possible light; and reel customers in because you've excited them about you and your product, service, or cause.

Here's the Real Deal

- Play angel's advocate: Visualize positive outcomes, which increases the likelihood of making them happen.

- Be your own Barnum & Bailey: With unbridled enthusiasm get people pumped up about what it is you are selling.

- It's so simple (ISS) steps take away the fear of pitching and give you confidence to present your pitch.

Chapter 9

Let's Perk-O-Late a Deal

True generosity requires more of us than kindly impulse. Above all it requires imagination—the capacity to see people in all their perplexities and needs, and to know how to expend ourselves effectively for them.

—I.A.R. Wylie

L et's assume that, at this point, you know you have their favorable attention. In fact, you're confident that you are close to securing the deal. Is there some type of perk you can add, delete, change, or tweak that will be the difference between being a deal maker or a deal breaker?

Perk-O-Late your deals by offering that little something extra. That special touch or added bonus can seal the deal in more ways than one. Flexibility is the key phrase in Perk-O-Lating your close. You want to be able to think and act on your feet, quickly and with authority, so you can respond to changing circumstances adroitly.

Here's an example of a quick-thinking connection that was made from the top down (go straight to the source of contact). I had just joined the National Speakers Association (NSA), and it didn't take me long to figure out that there was one person who appeared to be the top gun within our organization: Dr. Nido Qubein, CSP, CPAE, chairman of Great Harvest Bread Company, currently president of High Point University, author of several sales books, including *Stairway to Success, How to Be a Great Communicator,* and *How to Be a Great Sales Professional.* Also, he's a sharp dresser and a handsome man. My introduction to him was made through a past president of the association who had come to speak to our local NSA chapter. I'd asked to sit next to Glenna Salsbury, CSP, CPAE, at lunch and we'd struck up a delightful friendship.

Glenna contacted me when she learned that Nido's wife had been diagnosed with breast cancer. Glenna asked if I could do her a favor by sending Nido one of my books. *One* of my books? Grateful to Glenna for this golden opportunity, I sent Nido a care package with everything my company produced—autographed, wrapped, and tied with a bow.

I enclosed a note saying that Glenna had asked me to send him these items and let him know that I hoped these products helped him and his family face a personal challenge. In return? Nido sent me a lifetime supply of his books, tapes, and programs. He's chosen me to speak at a foundation benefit that he chairs, and he has been a mentor ever since.

One of the points of this book is that when you follow its win-win-win steps, your connections keep paying off for you and everyone else long after you've made them. Several years later, I was attending our annual NSA convention. Nido had brought in Grammy award–winning entertainer Larry Gatlin. I was sitting too far back in the auditorium of 1,000-plus people to do anything about it that day, but I thought to myself, "Wouldn't it be cool to meet Larry Gatlin?"

Almost one year later I opened the local newspaper and saw that Larry was coming to town. He was the headliner in a play called *The Civil War* and was going to be in town for almost a week.

I immediately sent Nido an e-mail, asking if he could make arrangements to have Larry call me while he was in town. (Remember: Don't forget to ask!) I wanted to ask him to be the key celebrity and entertainment in our annual golf tournament. I knew Larry was an avid golfer, often playing in celebrity pro-ams. Weeks went by, and I didn't hear from Nido. On the day Larry's play was scheduled to begin, my telephone rang. "Christine, this is Nido. I apologize for not calling you sooner. I've been out of the country. I don't have time to talk right now because I'm going into a meeting, but Larry Gatlin is going to be calling you. Good-bye!"

I no sooner hung up when the phone rang again. In the deepest Texas twang I have ever heard came the words, "Christine, this is Larry Gatlin. I don't know who you are or why I'm calling you, but Nido Qubein asked me to and anything Nido says, I do. So who *are* you?" I started talking as fast as I could (wrong technique for closing the deal), explaining my golf tournament, and finally asking if he would consider being our key celebrity in next year's event.

There was a long pause, and then Larry continued. "Christine, I need to be honest with you here. I am a recovering alcoholic. I spent years of my life throwing away my money and my time. I have only two objectives at this point in my life, and one is to spend as much time as possible with my family. Did I tell you I have a brand-new baby granddaughter? And the other objective I have is that when I'm not home with my family, I need to be on the road making money for my band and me. By the way . . . what is the cause of your tournament?"

Well, I had been so nervous and excited that all I had focused on was trying to convince him to say "yes." I had not explained what the deal was all about! When I told Larry I was a breast cancer survivor trying to make money for research, there was another long pause.

"You know, Christine, I'm a survivor, too. Certainly not from the type of adversity you have faced, but a survivor nonetheless. But I'm sorry, Christine. I get invited to play in hundreds of these types of events every year, and I just can't take the time from my income and my family."

Let's stop and assess what has transpired up to this point:

1. I had made an excellent connection by getting to know Nido through Glenna, then having Nido set up the proper introduction to Larry. (Win)

2. In my haste to get what *I* wanted, I didn't introduce my proposition in a compelling way; in fact, I failed to state the worthwhile purpose of my request. (Lose)

3. I was too busy thinking about *our* needs (an entertainer who can play golf) and ignored Larry's needs (time and money). (Lose)

Let's Perk-O-Late a Deal

I was at two strikes, but I wasn't out completely. As I wrote in Chapter 1, I never take the first "no" as the final "no." I did exactly what I am encouraging you to try: I followed the three Rs (retreat, reevaluate, and reapproach). This time there was a long pause, but it was from me.

"Larry, you've said that one of your objectives is to spend more time with your family. I know nothing about your personal life [an error on my part that can often lose the deal], but what would you think if I flew your wife, your kids, and your new baby granddaughter to Minneapolis to be with you for a few days?"

I had just talked Sun Country Airlines into donating 10 round-trip airline tickets to our event. If we had to use them to get Larry Gatlin, we could and we would. Another long pause . . . then, laughter.

"Well, Christine, I've got to be honest with you now. No one has *ever* made me an offer like that! And I have to be truthful again—my baby granddaughter is six months old. I don't think she'd enjoy flying to Minneapolis!"

I still wouldn't take "no" for an answer yet. I knew that Larry's second objective was money. We had money in our budget for celebrities; we'd just never had to use it before. So I offered, "Larry, how about if I pay you to come and play in our golf tournament?"

"Now you're talking, woman! Bring your marketing kit and any other information you have down to the Grand Hotel where I'm staying. I'll take a look." (Win-win-win!)

Close Basket

With a few hours to spare, I flew into high gear. I drove all around town collecting things to put into a gift basket to create a killer marketing kit. I wanted to knock Larry's socks off. Let's see . . . What would he like—no, love?

I wasn't acting blindly; I had a profile on Larry. He was an entertainer, Grammy winner, husband, father, grandfather, brother, Texan, recovering alcoholic, golfer, and provider.

I drove to my golf club and asked the golf pro if I could possibly get a dozen of the brand-new, hot-off-the-rack Pro V1s by Titleist. The balls had just been featured the day before on the front page of the sports section in *USA Today* as the "I have to have that" thing. Our head pro, Doug Nelson, told me that the club had sold out its supply in a day.

Committed to making this work, I told Doug what I was doing. Because Doug helped run our tournament, he was sympathetic. He took me into his private office, opened his bottom drawer, and there in the drawer was one, lone box of PRO V1s . . . his "private stash."

Doug made a sacrifice and let me buy the balls, and then I found a tiny pink pair of leather baby golf shoes for Larry's granddaughter. I attached a note that said, "I hope you grow up to be a great golfer like your granddad." I found a copy of *Chicken Soup for the Golfer's Soul* and autographed the page where I had submitted a story. Gourmet coffee, top-of-the-line chocolates—this gift basket was ready to boogie! I raced down to the hotel where Larry was staying, dropped off the gift basket and a copy of our tournament's marketing kit, and paid the concierge to personally deliver the basket to Larry's room (playing angel's advocate to ensure that Larry got the basket).

The next morning, my phone rang again. "Christine, this is Larry. This is quite an event you put on, young lady. I will not only play in your tournament, but I will come in the night before and entertain your guests, and I am lookin' forward to it. By the way, would you like two front-row tickets to Friday night's performance? We can meet for coffee and dessert after the show. And where in the heck did you happen to find these Titleist Pro V1s? You are amazing!"

Larry played in our tournament; in fact, his team won the event. We raised more money than ever before—more than $270,000. He entertained our audience beyond our wildest imaginations (exceeding our expectations). He and I struck up a working relationship that has lasted for many years, and I consider him a wonderful friend.

Let's think about what transpired this time:

1. I didn't take the first "no" as a final "no." In fact, I didn't even take the second "no" as final.

2. I followed the three Rs (retreat, reevaluate, and reapproach).

3. I listened to Larry's needs and addressed them immediately.

4. I Perk-O-Lated the deal in several ways (tickets for his family, compensation for his time, the gift basket). In other words, I spent money to make money.

5. I established a favorable impression by going all out and taking care of all the details (played angel's advocate).

6. I perfected the tailored close (a close created just for Larry) by creating the compelling pitch that had Larry saying, "I have to have that."

Let's look at some additional ways *you* can Perk-O-Late *your* deals. Perks are those special something extras that are unexpected: a bonus, tip, gratuity, or surprise that can make the difference between "Let me think about this" to "Let's close a deal!"

In general, it's always nice to underpromise and overdeliver. Perks can help you achieve that and can also keep existing customers coming back for more. For example, if someone orders something from The Cancer Club, such as a book, we insert a bookmark with a beautiful poem on it in their package and give them a copy of the most current Cancer Club newsletter. The intent is that when they open their package, their feeling would be, "Wow, I wasn't expecting that!" It's a little added bonus that costs us pennies but adds a touch of something extra to what they already purchased.

Another example would be when I speak for an organization, I donate a full set of my books to be used as door prizes, to put in their internal library, or simply for them to read and enjoy. This doesn't cost me much, but it's an unexpected bonus.

These, of course, are perks I'm adding after I've already made the sale. Unexpected bonuses add an element of surprise. But what if you're trying to close the deal? How do perks come in handy? By adding a little something extra, the majority of people will believe they are getting more bang for their buck. They will believe that there is value added to their original purchase.

You can look at the products and services you provide to decide whether there is something within your own company's inventory that can be added during the negotiations. This is often the least expensive way of adding value. Or you can search outside your company or organization for something that will complement your product or service. With new product introductions—before people become familiar with your product or service—you may want to add a perk that ties in to what it is you're selling. For example, if you are selling a new kind of ball washer to golf courses, your perk could be a sleeve of balls. If you're selling lawn services, a rake or shovel could help you close the deal. If you have just opened a hair waxing salon, you may offer a free massage following a waxing.

Perks don't have to be expensive, but even the smallest perk will be perceived as a gift or bonus. That's not to say that you shouldn't invest in your perks. Remember: It takes money to make money. The first year I started our Divorcing Divas conferences (and no one knew who we were or what we were all about), I offered to do a free speech for the company that came on board as our presenting sponsor. Technically, this didn't cost me a dime outside of my valuable time. But to the client, it seemed like an enormous gift, and it helped me close the deal.

Hosting both a fund-raising golf tournament and an all-day educational conference for Divorcing Divas has taught me a great deal about perks. As we try to solicit sponsors and vendors, I've been forced to answer the questions: "What would they want or like in exchange for their monetary contribution? What would they *love?*" Our marketing kits outline the benefits or perks of their contribution, based on their level of participation: industry exclusivity, the opportunity to present one of the keynote presentations or one or more breakout sessions, articles in our monthly e-newsletter, ads in our event program, a link from our website to theirs, premier seating at the event, multiple foursomes for the golf tournament, and on and on.

Ask yourself, in addition to the product or service I'm selling, what would they love? We can't all be catering to professional athletes and captains of commerce whose perks exceed our wildest imaginations: private jets, signing bonuses, country club privileges, or exclusive housing accommodations. But we can sweeten the deal by something as simple as taking our prospects to lunch or dinner, treating them to 50-yard line tickets at a football game or a round of golf, inviting them to a play or concert, or giving them tickets to the Children's Theater.

These gestures or perks give a clear message: I am investing in you and our relationship. Your business is important to me. I want you to be happy; no, more than happy: I want you to be thrilled. I want you to be surprised!

When I was working for SPAR Marketing, every year one of my customers, Toys 'R' Us, hosted an annual event to thank *its* customers and vendors. We'd each be assigned a booth to display our goods and services. It was a several-day event that included golfing, dining, and schmoozing outside the walls of its building in Paramus, New Jersey. This particular year, the event was being held in Florida.

I thought to myself, "What can I do that will really knock their socks off in terms of separating myself from all the other vendors and service providers?" Over the years I had developed a hobby of attending the U.S. Open Golf Tournaments. I went to 23 consecutive tournaments and, as a result, had had the privilege of meeting several of the professional golfers, their caddies, and their families. The late Bruce Edwards, caddy for Tom Watson, had become a good friend.

I knew Bruce lived in Florida, and I gave him a call. "What would you think about coming to our event, positioning yourself in my booth, and offering putting lessons to everyone who stops by the booth?" (A win for me and a win for Toys 'R' Us.)

Bruce hesitated. Although he had the time available to attend the event, it was across the state, he'd need hotel accommodations, and it was time away from home. "I'll pay you for your time and expenses," I said immediately, Perk-O-Lating the deal. I didn't know if SPAR would be willing to cover the expense I had just racked up, but I knew that Toys 'R' Us was a big enough account for me that, if necessary, I was willing to absorb the cost. Bruce responded, "I'll be there on Tuesday." It goes without saying that our booth was the most popular booth at the show. From the chief executive officer (CEO) of Toys 'R' Us, the company's buyers, and other vendors and suppliers, everyone wanted a chance to learn how to putt from Bruce. Bruce passed away at an early age from amyotrophic lateral sclerosis, but I'll never forget his warm smile, friendly face, and kind heart. Thanks, Bruce!

Never go on a sales call without some type of perk or bonus you can add to the pot if the deal is turning sour. If you need to obtain permission ahead of time from your company or your supervisor, get it so you don't have to stop in the middle of your pitch to say, "Let me call my office and see if I can get you a little something more." You want to be in a position of authority to make decisions to help drive your business.

In the negotiation process, the addition of a perk should be a last-ditch effort to finalize the sale. We've all experienced that when buying a new car, home, washing machine, or any other major purchase. Usually the perk comes in the form of money off. With major purchases, we half expect that perk to happen. But if you're negotiating for a two-year service contract with a major supplier and you feel the sale slipping away, say something such as, "I've heard your concerns and hesitation, Ted. How about if we add your own custom project manager to the contract at no extra cost? Would this exclusive arrangement be enough for you to close our deal?"

It may be that you were planning to do that anyway if the contract was large enough. But just extending some sort of benefit or add-on can be the difference between shaking the prospect's hand and watching him or her walk away.

Perk-O-Lating the deal is a fun, creative, and imaginative way of closing deals. As Jimmy Fallon says on those Capital One commercials, "What's in *your* wallet?"

Here's the Real Deal

- Perk-O-Late your deals by offering that little something extra.

- Underpromise and overdeliver using perks to achieve that.

- Perks can come from inside or outside your organization.

- Perks don't have to be expensive.

- Be in a position of authority to offer perks to help drive your business.

Chapter 10

Let's Ask for a Deal

If you don't ask, you don't get.

—Mahatma Gandhi

Fess up. Have you ever sent out a great proposal that you put a lot of effort into . . . and then not followed up with a call? Think about it. How many solicited materials have *you* received through the mail or the Internet and never heard from the person who sent them to you?

I call this the throw-everything-at-the-wall theory. It's based on the fact that we don't concentrate long enough on any one proposal or sale. Instead of waiting to see what sticks, we are already moving on to the next potential opportunity. Unfortunately, too many of the things we throw out there don't get closed because we simply never asked for the business. Don't forget to ask! This is one of the most important components of closing the deal. The worst thing people will say is "no." The best things can come back to you in spades.

Close String Budget

Many of us dream of expanding our businesses or maybe even starting up our own. But as with any expansion or start-up, we are usually limited by two key components: time and capital.

Because most of us are not independently wealthy, and the late Ed McMahon never came knocking on our doors on Super Bowl Sunday, we often get caught in the middle: We can't afford to expand or start up, yet we can't afford not to if we seriously mean business.

That's where the phase "penny for your thoughts" comes to mind. If people were willing to pay a penny for our thoughts, would they be willing to pay $1, $10, $100, or more? Most of us have probably never stopped to ask ourselves the question, "Would people be willing to help me if I only asked? And how much would they be willing to give?"

This thought process was taken to heart five months after I started my first business, The Cancer Club. The basics had been done to at least outwardly appear as if I had a viable company. I had purchased business cards and stationery, set up my phone and fax, registered my company's name, purchased its trademark, created a logo, and so on, but I just didn't have the nest egg I needed to quit my real job and focus on my dream full time.

So I sat down and wrote the "ask" letter. In the letter I gave a compelling opening statement. I outlined the mission statement of my company and explained why I was starting it, what I hoped to achieve, who I hoped to reach, and how I hoped to get there. And then I asked the million-dollar question: "Would you be willing to consider a gift to help me get my business off the ground?"

I addressed the letter to 500 people: family, business associates, neighbors, and acquaintances. I made it clear that although my company was not a nonprofit organization, for any contribution they made, 50 percent would be donated back to a nonprofit, cancer-related cause.

The moment I dropped the letters in the mailbox, I slid down to the sidewalk, clutching the mailbox with every ounce of strength I had. I went crawling back on my hands and knees to the Postmaster General begging to let me take the letters back. *What had I done?* I couldn't believe I'd asked people for money!

I was in total despair until the very next day, when the first check for $10 was in my mailbox from a neighbor I barely knew. He and his wife had attached a note saying, "Go for it, Christine!" The next day brought another, and the next day another, until within two months I received more than $20,000 in gifts and words of encouragement.

For those who didn't want to give me cash (after all, my company was a for-profit organization), I received offers of free services such as printing, secretarial help, computer expertise, and photography. I, in turn, tried to come up with unique ways to give appreciation and recognition for each of the services rendered. For example, in our company newsletter, I had a special section to acknowledge all of the donations for the printing, illustrations, and photography. I highlighted their gifts and published their phone numbers and business names as free advertising for them and their services.

My company has been thriving and expanding on a daily, weekly, and monthly basis since 1995 thanks to hard work, determination, and a *lot* of help from my friends. It was a risk I took, but in the long run, it was well worth the effort.

Many months later I was sitting on my deck with a close friend who owns 13 stores in a national franchise. For whatever reason she had not chosen to make a contribution of time, money, or services to my company when she had received my original "ask" letter. She broached the subject by saying, "You know, Christine, I wish people would have given *me* money when I first started my own business 11 years ago." My response was, "Did you ever ask anyone?" Could your dream become reality if you drummed up the courage to ask for help?

Ask for Help to Close the Deal

Why don't a lot of us ask for help or ask for the sale? We're afraid of rejection. We're afraid of failure. But rather than anticipating rejection and failure, we need to set ourselves up so that we cannot fail. How do we do that?

First, make a list of every possible objection a prospect or client might have. From the smallest complaint to the largest challenge, approach your deal with the confidence that you can answer any question or solve any problem that may be thrown your way.

If possible, offer a buffet of options for your prospects and clients. Maybe they can't afford your fully loaded package of goods or services, but perhaps they could get started on a smaller scale. Perhaps you could offer them a trial period, a fully refundable investment, or a payment plan. By setting up a buffet of options, you are giving your prospects and customers choices. You are saying, "I'm not inflexible. I care enough about you and your business to bend the rules to accommodate *your* needs." Your buffet of options may be tiered pricing based on quantity; speed of delivery based on deadlines; the option to be "first"; or first right of refusal. We can offer all kinds of options if we are ready to ask for the order.

When asking for the order, you want to be clear whose territory you are in: yours or theirs. If you have a product or service that someone cannot do without (an example here would be a recall of a product and the company needs to do damage control immediately), you are in your territory. Your prospect needs *your* service or *your* product, and they need it fast. Usually we are on the *other* side of the fence: Your product or service would be nice to have, but we don't necessarily *need* it. If you have a clear understanding of where you stand before you ask for the deal, you are more likely to be successful.

Daniel B. Ahlberg, MD, is a retired neurosurgeon who learned the value of establishing territories at a relatively young age. After completing his postgraduate medical education and residency, he was ready to start practicing. He had only one problem: There wasn't an opening in town for a neurosurgeon. So Dr. Dan decided to set up his own private practice.

Dr. Dan hustled back in the day. He joined the staff of nearly every hospital in town, introducing himself to the other doctors in hospital emergency rooms, break rooms, and hospital cafeterias. As years passed, Dr. Dan's neurosurgical practice grew and became very successful. Partners were hired to help expand the practice.

At the same time Dr. Dan's practice was growing and thriving, so were the hospitals in the area. One in particular wanted to establish itself as a Level 1 Trauma Center. The criteria were stringent, and a partnership with a neurosurgical practice was critical to their success. Approaching Dr. Dan, he agreed to sign a one-year contract to provide the administrative services required.

Dr. Dan was doing his research, however, and in other parts of the country, hospitals were paying the doctors a per diem for being on call at Level 1 hospitals. He went back to the drawing board knowing the hospital couldn't succeed without him and his practice and successfully negotiated a five-year contract with a generous per diem, a full-time dedicated nurse practitioner, and many other benefits for him and his practice. The Level 1 hospital thrived.

Five years later, when the contract was up for renewal, Dr. Dan was in the driver's seat. He not only doubled the length of the contract to 10 years, but he doubled the price of the per diem and the other benefits, too.

Most of us don't think of doctors as salespeople. When asked about his success as a negotiator, Dr. Dan says, "Do your research. Know where your strengths are, and most importantly, understand *need*. Determine if you're negotiating from a position of strength or weakness. Accurately understand the situation, and then negotiate accordingly."

The "ask" requires that you have developed a sense of trust with this person or organization. Think back on the processes you've put in place to get to this point: You planted a seed in a garden that had not yet existed or blossomed by making initial contact and perhaps sending out samples or materials. You analyzed the timing, pricing, competition, feasibility, and expectations and looked at this sale as "What's in it for three? Who is the third-party beneficiary here who will benefit from our connection?" You've been reliable and presentable. You know whose territory you are in. And though you may not have a track record yet with this prospect or client, you have developed a trust factor.

When I was diagnosed with breast cancer, I interviewed surgeons as stringently as I would have interviewed candidates for president of the United States. I was diagnosed on December 19, so my week before Christmas that year was full of doctors' appointments and decisions.

I had not yet made up my mind regarding who should do my surgery and decided to give my emotions a rest for a few days over the holidays. On Christmas night my telephone rang. "Christine, this is Dr. Margaret Bretzke. You and I met in my offices earlier this week. I'm not calling for any reason other than to ask you how you're doing. This must be a very difficult holiday for you this year."

I made my decision then and there. Dr. Bretzke made a sacrifice that evening: She took valuable time away from her family on a holiday to call me to see how I was doing. She immediately solidified my trust in her and showed how she would treat me as a patient. I not only hired her as my surgeon, I have recommended her to hundreds of cancer patients since. It's no surprise that some years later, she was featured on the front cover of *Mpls. St. Paul Magazine* as "Top Doctor" in the Twin Cities.

What else can you do to establish trust?

To inspire confidence you can bring or provide references—lots of them. You can also deliver a return on investment analysis. You can share case studies of other satisfied customers. And never promise what you cannot deliver.

Close Line

There are different ways to ask for a sale. Try on some of these closes:

- "Kevin, we've been talking about having you come on board as a client for about six months now. I believe we have a great fit and that I can do a lot to help you advance your business. I'd like to see if we can solidify our proposal. Are you ready to move forward?"

- "Carla, I can't think of a better person I'd rather do business with. You and I seem to have extremely compatible values and beliefs about our respective companies, and I believe I have a lot to offer you. I'd really like to move forward. May I ask you for your business?"

- "Tom, I've been demonstrating my new product to you for several months. In that period of time we've had terrific feedback, made some minor improvements, and gotten quite a bit of publicity. I'd really like for you to be one of the first to use our product. Can I write up an order for you now?"

Trying on different styles of closing can help you become comfortable with the words you are using. It can help you build confidence. If you have success with one type of close, then use it again. Keep in mind, though, that not everyone responds in the same way. That's why it's important for you to read and understand what your prospect or client is saying to you: From the person's body language to his or her response time, to the tone in the person's voice, all of these are clues and cues as to the quality of your pitch. So what are some of the signs or clues to look for?

They Love Me

Everyone gives off some type of vibe when being sold to. The key is in being able to read that vibe. What are the signs of a good vibe?

- Your client or prospect seems genuinely glad to see you or takes your call. If you reach voice mail, your call is returned within 24 hours.

- Your client or prospect continues to ask questions or ask for additional information about your product or service.

- Your client or prospect asks to meet others involved with your company and/or organization or asks you if you would be willing to meet with others in his or her organization.

- Your client or prospect calls *you.*

All of these are positives that should translate into further conversation and/or negotiations that will hopefully result in a done deal. In all of these cases, you have the permission to keep things moving forward. Dialogue in this case should look something like, "Karin, you seem genuinely interested in my service contract. I'd like to see if we can reach an agreement and start moving forward. Would you be able to meet for lunch anytime this week?"

But what are some cues that your client or prospect isn't interested? It's just as important to read those signs so that you don't come across as one of those pushy, pesky, obnoxious, demanding salespeople.

- The administrative assistant says your client or prospect is in the office initially but comes back and tells you he or she is in a meeting. You don't get a return phone call.
- Your client or prospect makes lots of excuses as to why he or she can't buy what it is you have to offer.
- The conversation turns to the client or prospect telling you everything that is wrong with your product, service, or cause.
- Your client or prospect asks for a better deal.
- Your client or prospect tells you he or she has gone with a competitor.

In each of these scenarios, something you've done has turned the person off. You can ask:

- "Ed, can you tell me if something I did or said has caused you some concern about doing business with me?"
- "Caroline, have I left out any details about my product that have prevented you from making a firm decision?"
- "Jeffrey, is there any additional information or questions I might be able to answer that would give you a better understanding of how we'd move forward with this sale?"

If you've gotten to this point, go back and reread Chapter 1. Just because the person has said "no" *today* doesn't mean he or she won't say "yes" in another year. So stop sitting in your cubicle or your home office shuffling papers and straightening your desk. Gather your courage, and don't forget to ask!

Here's the Real Deal

- Instead of anticipating rejection, set yourself up so you cannot fail.

- Offer a buffet of options for prospects and clients.

- Be clear whose territory you are in: yours or theirs.

- The "ask" requires you to develop a sense of trust.

- Try on different closes to become comfortable with your words.

- Don't forget to ask!

Section IV

Uh, Oh . . . No Deal?

Remember that a prospect must buy you before he buys your product.

—Anonymous

Chapter 11

Let's Not Ruin the Deal

H as anyone ever been pitching you a product when one tiny thing that person said or did changed your mind? Have you ever been pitching a deal when you suddenly realized, "I've lost them"? What are the irritating things we do as salespeople that turn us from deal makers into deal breakers?

Let's take a look at some of the scenarios that can ruin our deals:

- You don't follow up.
- You change the parameters.
- You don't know when to quit.
- You take or give credit where credit isn't due.
- You put down the competition.
- You have no flexibility.
- You're judgmental.
- You promised something you can't deliver.
- You can't address their concerns because you don't have enough information, permission, knowledge, or ability to think quickly on your feet.
- You have not established a sense of "I have to have that."
- You said or did something they considered in bad taste.
- You appeared cocky or overconfident.
- You didn't prepare properly.

Close-out Sale

We had been in conversations with Bic Corporation to merchandise its pens in retail outlets such as Target, Kmart, and Wal-Mart when company representatives asked to come tour our offices. I made sure we had fresh coffee and rolls, and I was going to pick them up at the airport. I had their proposals printed in beautiful binders, and I had all the executives from my firm ready to meet theirs. I forgot one tiny detail, however.

When we got to our offices and sat down in the boardroom, I pulled a pen out of my purse to take notes. The name on the pen? Paper Mate.

I tried to hide it and slipped out of the room, but the damage had already been done. No deal.

Just as in the previous chapter where it was explained how to read the clues to determine whether someone is interested, there are also clues you can use to tell if the person you are pitching to is changing his or her mind. These are situations where your contact has previously exhibited all the signs of interest—you've met or spoken by phone or e-mail dozens of times and you generally believe you are going to close the deal—when all of a sudden something has gone wrong.

- The person suddenly starts to backpedal, saying that the timing isn't right or there's no money in the budget for this year.

- The person compliments you profusely but goes on to say that, although you did a terrific job presenting your product or service, he or she has decided they don't need what you have to offer.

- The prospect shares with you that talks are also ongoing with other vendors or salespeople.

- The person tell you that, if given the power to decide, he or she would purchase; however, the boss, superior, committee, or board has decided to look at other options.

A failed deal can have repercussions that ripple throughout a business or organization. And although these types of losses happen to everyone, the first step to fixing a collapsing deal is spotting the change when it happens. Just as you need to have your antennae and feelers up when looking for new business in all the wrong places, you need to be just as alert to spot changes in behavior or habits. Reading and adjusting to these clues and cues can salvage a deal going wrong at just the right time.

We have forty million reasons for failure, but not a single excuse.

—Rudyard Kipling

He Came That Close . . .

Paul Magers was the most popular TV news anchor on our NBC affiliate, KARE 11, for almost 20 years. As the most watched man in Minnesota, he was as warm and friendly in public as he was on TV. For five years we were blessed to have him volunteer to serve as the master of ceremonies for our golf tournament. When he wasn't volunteering or playing golf, he was helping KARE 11 maintain its position as the number-one news station in our area.

As much as he had created Niche Notoriety for himself and his station, even more has been made over how the station lost him. Paul confirms that his agent was unable to get KARE 11 to the bargaining table until his contract (estimated at $11 million over 10 years) was close to expiring. Negotiations only started limping along when KARE 11 initially offered roughly a 10 percent raise. "After that," said Paul, "my conversations with other stations intensified." Trumpeting him as the potential next Dan Rather, KCBS-TV lured Paul to Los Angeles for what was rumored to be almost double his salary.

How did KARE 11 lose their star? Where did this deal get ruined?

Paul claims that if they had just expressed interest, started the negotiations earlier, or paid any attention to him, he would have stayed in Minnesota.

Let's Not Ruin the Deal

After all, money isn't everything. His family was grounded there; his daughters were in the local schools, and all his good friends—and his wife's friends—lived in the area. The list of pluses for staying with his home station far outweighed the list of minuses—2 to 1.

However, more than Paul's job was at stake (lose-lose-lose). It's a classic case of dropping the ball, and it happens to us every day. They didn't treat him with the respect he deserved. As a result, he moved on. Let's talk about ways we can pick up that ball instead of dropping it so we don't ruin situations that should be done deals.

One way to start is by analyzing your sales efforts that have failed. Is there a pattern here that you can identify? At what point of the negotiation process do things start to fall apart? Is it consistent, or is it something different every time?

If necessary, seek outside help or opinions. This is where a mentor or mentors come in handy. Seek tough love. Ask of others, "What might I be doing that perhaps turns some people off?" Is this a behavior you can change or modify?

Asking people for help is one of the best things you can do for your career or your life. People want to help you succeed and are usually honored that you've turned to them for advice.

Break bad habits (interrupting, justifying, ignoring, pleading, forgetting, etc.) by identifying your shortcomings. You're educated. They're educated. Yet it happens every day. Someone mispronounces a word, and you feel the need to correct him or her. Don't. "Nitch" instead of "niche" (rhymes with *quiche*); "forté" instead of "forte" (it's only one syllable, not two, depending on its use) "Her Mess" instead of "Hermès."

Correcting others will only make them feel badly, possibly stupid, and definitely inferior. Instead, bone up on your own vocabulary by reading, studying other cultures, and listening to the educators. They're only words, after all, and you get the message.

Work your weaknesses instead of focusing on your strengths. I am a fairly decent golfer, sporting a 14.2 USGA handicap. Every single time I go to the practice range to hit balls, I bring the same four clubs: my 8 and 6 irons, my 3 wood, and my driver.

As I perch myself on the range and hit balls, I hear over and over, "Christine, what a great swing you have!" That's because I have perfected these four clubs and what they can do for me. But the reason I'm still a 14 and not in the single digits is because I never work my weaknesses. I never go to the practice putting green or the chip-and-pitch area of the practice facilities. So what happens to me when I get out on the golf course? I chuck a 30-foot shot onto the green into the sand trap. I send a 10-foot putt 4 feet past the hole. Why? Because even though I know I should be working on my weaknesses, I continue to do what makes me feel good. The reality, however, is that I often feel terrible about myself after a round of golf because I've made so many horrible mistakes!

Part of how we become better salespeople—and golfers—is that we make it a priority—a goal—to get better. Pick up the ball instead of dropping it by changing your behavior. Take lessons or hire a coach. Enroll in classes or participate in online education. Read books. Study the masters. But do one thing: Change your close.

So what's the last thing that can ruin your deals? People who don't want you to succeed. These can include former bosses, colleagues, or even total strangers. How do you prevent this from happening? By keeping these people close to the vest.

Choose Your Friends . . . and Your Enemies

Ty Votaw spent seven successful years as the commissioner of the LPGA. Volatile, controversial, and ever evolving, the job had its challenges. Ty remembers something his father said to him that came back to him again and again. "In equal parts cynical and cautionary, he once said to me, 'Good friends come and go, but a good enemy can last you a lifetime.'"

Ty continues, "The fact is that while you hope you can stay in touch with and be good friends to the people you consider your friends in life, the reality is that—unfortunately—you do lose touch and are not always there for them (or they for you). But having a universe of friends does make your life richer and fuller. Conversely, it seems the people who, for some reason, have become your enemies come in and out of your life at unforeseen moments to wreak havoc on your plans or fortunes."

Choose your friends and enemies well. Or better still, have as many friends and as few enemies as you possibly can. You'd never want them to ruin your deals.

Here's the Real Deal

- The first step to fixing a collapsing deal is spotting change when it happens.

- Analyze your sales efforts that have failed.

- Ask people for help.

- Break bad habits by identifying your shortcomings.

- Work your weaknesses.

- Choose your friends and enemies well.

Chapter 12

Let's R-R-Reapproach the Deal

W e've discussed the value of backing off, assessing our situation, and rethinking our options with the three Rs: retreat, reevaluate, and reapproach. In our dreams, deals are opened and closed and always work out just the way we envision. In the real world, that's not always the case. It's rare for a buyer to turn to you and say, "I'll take it!" on the first try. Learning the tools to retreat, reevaluate, and reapproach can be the difference between permanently losing a deal or just temporarily losing a deal.

Let's think about the previous chapter for a moment. Your prospect is losing interest or has simply told you he or she doesn't want what you have to offer. Now is the time to retreat. It may be helpful to notify your prospect or client that you're about to do that. "Kevin, I need some time to give this more thought. I've heard some concerns and issues in our conversations, and I need about a week to see if I can truly find the solutions and answers you deserve."

Retreat

By giving prospects notice that you're dropping out of the picture—albeit temporarily—you have indicated that you still are interested in them and that you want to do what is best for them. Too often we drop off the face of the Earth and our prospects think, "I know I wasn't jumping up and down about that new product Kevin had to offer, but I was *somewhat* interested. I wonder what ever happened to him."

During the retreat phase, literally sit and write down everything that has led you to this point of the negotiations. Ask yourself: What have I done right? What might I have done wrong? Have I heard everything they had to say or ask about my product or service? Did I answer all the questions my prospect has asked thus far?

This is an excellent time to seek outside counsel. "Sherry, I have a prospect, and I was fairly confident he was going to do business with me, but something has changed and I just can't quite put my finger on what is going wrong. Can you spare me a few minutes to go over what has transpired so far? I really respect you and your opinion. And I'll buy the coffee!"

During the retreat phase, you can still drop your prospect or client a quick e-mail saying, "I haven't forgotten about you. I'm still working on solutions. I will be in touch soon." Taking a break, however long or short, gives you time to rethink your process and plan your reapproach. It may shed some light on what might have gone wrong. It gives you time to regroup.

So you're going to back off for a couple of months. Now what? It's time to reevaluate. This process should begin immediately while conversations and interactions are still fresh in your mind. Have you ever had to write a paper for school, a publication, or a white paper for a client and you develop writer's block? So it is with everything in life. Sometimes we need to step back, take a deep breath, stretch, and notice that there's a different path we can take.

Reevaluate

During the reevaluate period, you need to dig deep to answer the question, "What is going wrong?" The truth to the matter is that we may never know the reasons why some relationships work out and others fail, but if it's happening to you often, something is amiss. It can be small things: "Beth showed up wearing yoga pants, and it was really distracting," or "Christine had this tiny little green piece of salad dangling from her tooth the entire time she was presenting. It was really gross and disgusting."

Or it can be larger things such as, "Susan showed up 15 minutes late for our appointment this morning, and it threw me off for the rest of my day." Often these tiny details are things that we could have controlled. Take a complete physical inventory of yourself before you meet with somebody, and try to be on time. If you are running late, by all means call and let them know. If I'm going to be even 5 minutes late I always make my contact aware of the situation. Procter & Gamble taught me well: "If you're not 5 minutes early, you're 5 minutes late."

Here are some things you can examine:

- **Your appearance:** Give yourself a complete physical inventory, from what you wear, to your perfume or cologne, to your hair and your nails. Ask yourself, could something I've worn be perceived as offensive to someone else? If you have to stop to think, the answer is probably "yes." Business is always a good time to be conservative. It's not a good time to be showing off cleavage, chest hair, or anything else you'd find in a dance club.

- **Your approach:** Ask yourself if you're making yourself clear. Are you confident about the features and benefits of what you are selling? Are you knowledgeable? If you aren't feeling confident, gather the information you need and practice a different approach.

- **Your marketing materials and the things you've left behind with your prospect or client:** Are they current, modern, and state of the art, or do they look worn and outdated? It may be time to invest in that new marketing kit we talked about in Chapter 2.

By retreating and reevaluating, often you can clarify some mistakes you may have made or get clarity on something you might have done wrong. Now it's time to stand up, brush ourselves off, and try again!

Reapproaching someone who has turned you down is never easy. But hopefully, through the reevaluating period, you saw that clues and cues were dropped that you simply didn't pick up at the time. Now is the time to demonstrate that you really care about someone's business because you're not going to let that first "no" stop you from trying again.

Reapproach

I'm not saying this step is easy. It takes courage to reapproach someone. A good reapproach is simply to state fault or error. "Gregory, I know I made some mistakes the last time I called on you. I'm sorry for that. I've given it a lot of thought, and with your permission, I'd like the opportunity to meet or speak with you again. I believe I have some solid solutions to the concerns you expressed at our last meeting. May I buy you a cup of coffee?"

When reapproaching someone, keep these things in mind:

- People forgive easily. They generally *want* others to succeed. By stating fault and taking blame that things didn't go as planned the first time, you have opened the door for another chance.

- Your client or prospect may have been enthusiastic about your product or service in the first place, but then things fell apart. If your prospect is still interested, he or she will want to know what you might be able to do differently.

- Almost all of us have been in this boat. And because we can relate to this experience, we are sympathetic. I'm not advocating the sympathy factor, but if it works, go for it!

- Things may generally have changed for the better with your product's features, the direction of your company, or the length of time for delivery. If this is the case, you have every reason to toot your horn and try again.

I wouldn't have imagined that an eight-year-old child would have learned these skills at his young age, but then, the acorn never falls far from the tree. Here is a story about my son Brooks.

Fish Close!

Every year since my sons were little, it was a family tradition for us to take them to a marvelous resort in the north woods of Minnesota. The resort is appropriately named Grand View Lodge because of its spectacular perch overlooking majestic Gull Lake. We usually only stayed for a short three-night, four-day visit, but it was long enough for us to get away from the city, relax, and spend some quality time together.

We always went on the same weekend, stayed in the same cabin, and did almost the same things every year (loyals for life) in an effort to establish a sense of tradition that we hope our boys will carry on for many years to come. One of our days was spent with a fishing guide we'd hired and fishing to our heart's content (or the legal limit—whichever came first).

The year I was going through my treatments for cancer, I was particularly looking forward to our trip because I had already been through six months of chemotherapy and 33 days of radiation. I knew that Grand View would be just the thing to get my mind off my situation and help me focus on positive memories of days gone by and dreams of future years on the lake together with my family.

On the morning of our fishing excursion, the alarm went off at 5:30 so we could eat a hearty breakfast, get dressed, and be on the dock by 6:00 AM. It was a cloudy, overcast day—perfect for fishing. Our regular guide, Mark, showed up on time, and we took off for a day of delight.

"Mom," my youngest son, Brooks, who was eight at the time, asked, "are we having our annual contests?"

"You mean First Fish, Biggest Fish, and Most Fish?" asked Tim, eleven years old and already an experienced fisherman. "Ha, just watch! I'll win them all this year!"

Let the competition begin!

We found our first fishing hole, and with Mark's help, all hooks were baited and lines dropped. An hour went by without a nibble when Mark offered to move us to another part of the lake.

Eagerly, we dropped our lines in the quiet still of the morning, only a few signs of life starting to surface on the shore as cabin owners and guests started waking with the rising sun. Again, time sped quickly by and still not a bite. Hours passed as we would fish for a while, move to a new location, and try our luck again. You could see the disappointment on the boys' faces as the day turned into afternoon and nary a fish was to be seen.

Our guide apologized profusely for our bad luck and suggested we call it a day. Brooks, however, wasn't ready to take "no fish" as an answer. He asked, "Couldn't we cast one more line?" (Can't we pitch this one more time?) We agreed as I started putting away the remnants of lunch, packing up because it "wasn't our day."

Suddenly, Brooks screamed with delight. "I've hooked a big one!" We all eagerly watched and waited (biding our time) as he struggled to pull what appeared to be a keeper through the water. He pulled and reeled, all eyes on him when what should appear on the end of his line but the wig from the top of my head! I hadn't even noticed it was gone!

I gasped and reached to feel my baldness when the boys and the men burst into laughter. I could not help but laugh along with them as Brooks proudly removed my hair from his hook, turned to us, and announced, "It's a trifecta: First Fish, Biggest Fish, Most Fish—a clean sweep!" Brooks had "hooked" for business in all the wrong places!

Success is going from failure to failure without loss of enthusiasm.

—Winston Churchill

We laughed on the ride back to Grand View, the day's disappointments far from our thoughts. Twenty years have passed and we have continued our annual trips to Grand View Lodge. Every year on several occasions throughout the weekend someone will bring up that story, and we all laugh at the wonderful memory of the big one that got away (from my head).

Has your fishing expedition ever been like Brooks's? We didn't give up even though the day hadn't yielded any catches. We kept trying different places and techniques. Are you patient and tenacious enough to retreat, reevaluate, and reapproach? Even when we think it just isn't our day or that nothing is going right, we can turn a disaster into a victory by following this philosophy.

Instead of saying to yourself, "Rejection! Grr . . . ," say, "Rejection? RRR . . ."

So how do we retreat, reevaluate, and reapproach our contacts? First, we must choose graciousness over coercion. No one is going to respond well when we ourselves have come unglued. Always treat your prospects and customers with golden gloves. "It would be an honor and privilege to do business with you." Ask yourself, "Has there been any part of this process where I didn't act with the utmost professionalism?" Learn to consider rather than strong-arm. Everyone wants to be treated with honor and respect. You'll respect yourself more, too.

Ask yourself, "Did I listen hard enough? Did I hear everything my prospect had to say?"

Listeners Close Deals

As president of the Americas for MasterCard International, Ruth Ann Marshall traveled the globe creating partnerships that propelled MasterCard and the people she worked with to the top of their field.

A few years ago, I shared a house in Augusta, Georgia, during the Masters with Ruth Ann. Not long after, I asked her a question that often intrigues me about successful people: What experience in business taught her the most? As often is the case, Ruth Ann's response dealt with partnerships.

I spent several years as the COO and group executive president of Electronic Payment Services, a holding company that managed several prominent enterprises in the electronic payments industry.

141

At that point in the organization's history, I knew we had to take a quantum leap into the future by either going public or selling the company. We assessed the merits of both actions and decided on selling the company.

The process that followed was one of the most enlightening and expanding experiences I've ever had in my career. I led a cross-functional management team in assessing 16 different bids. Our criteria included many of the standard measures around financial resources, but we also put a strong emphasis on cultural attributes. Which of the suitors had the best cultural match to what our employees valued and expected?

Let's stop for a minute and explore how this relates to our businesses. Do we, as experts in our field, take the time to evaluate the cultural attributes of our potential customers? Are we seeking out clients who play into our area of expertise, or are we just taking business, despite the possibility of a misfit, just to have business?

Explore your potential customers' cultures to ensure that you are just the person to meet their needs. For example, I speak on using humor to overcome adversity. My niche is in health care. When I began my speaking career, because of my strong corporate background, companies I'd worked with in my previous job would ask me if I spoke on the use of humor in the workplace. Because I hadn't done my due diligence—I hadn't researched this culture thoroughly—I assumed that my message could transcend health care. I quickly learned I was wrong.

Ruth Ann continued, "We invited in a number of the suitors. Each would spend a few days with us. This was a great learning experience because I had to crawl through every facet of my company to be able to explain it to the potential bidders. The process taught me volumes. Most important, I learned the value of looking beyond price—to seek out a company that would be best on an ongoing basis for the people staying with EPS over the long term."

Price. How often does it drive your business? And should it? Turning down business because it truly isn't a fit is the right thing to do if what you have to offer does not fit the culture of your prospective suitor.

I also asked Ruth Ann what she learned as a young adult that helped her. Ruth Ann shared that she learned something from each of her parents.

One of my mother's favorite expressions is, "You have two ears and one mouth, which means you should listen twice as much as you speak." The value I derive from listening to customers, colleagues and employees is immense. And you can glean as much by what isn't said, as by what is. There is no substitute for listening if you want to learn.

That's hard advice to us as salespeople; we tend to speak first and listen later. Ruth Ann reminds us to let our clients do the talking. We're so busy selling ourselves that we haven't heard our client's needs, concerns, or preferences.

Ruth Ann continued, "My father was a prominent executive with AT&T for decades. He taught me that people do business with people they like and trust. This notion is put to the test in the modern age of e-mail and teleconferencing, but the foundation of business is still personal engagement and living up to your word. Everything I do is based on the trust of developing a relationship that will be long lasting beyond whatever short-term transaction I'm involved in at the moment."

Sometimes we have to retreat, reevaluate, and reapproach because the timing isn't right or the customer just isn't a fit . . . for the moment. You can choose your battles. We often hear that the smallest customers demand the most time, energy, focus, and so on, and sometimes the time, energy, and focus just aren't justified. In that case, you may make a decision to pass along that client or prospect to someone else in your firm or to the friendly competition. After all, there are only so many hours in our day.

You can learn to better qualify your buyers. Dig deep before you make a sales call to determine whether this person or company is a "close" hanger or a contact who tries on "close"? In other words, will this person or company become a staple in my closet and be a loyal for life, or is this person just wasting my time, trying to drive down our price or get additional features and benefits we don't usually offer?

Some think it's holding on that makes one strong; sometimes it's letting go.

—Sylvia Robinson

The Door Is Closed

So let's say after all this effort, your prospect simply turns you down. What should you do? Ask the person *why* you lost his or her business. "May I ask, who did you give your business to and what could I have done differently to secure your business?" The person's answers can be invaluable toward improving your pitch for future sales calls.

Sometimes it is best to simply let go. We can never be all things to all people. Some deals aren't meant to be. If you are feeling so frustrated and anxious that you're not closing a certain deal, it's probably time to walk away. But hopefully you learned a few things, walked away graciously by thanking your prospect for the opportunity to bid on the business, and can look yourself in the eye and say in your loudest voice, "Next!"

Last, you can simply establish patience as your virtue. "I didn't succeed this time with my approach, but I know I'll succeed next time with the valuable information I learned from this experience." Save face and get back in the race. As Brooks proved that one summer day, "There are lots of fish in this pond."

Here's the Real Deal

- Notify your prospect that you are going to retreat.

- During the retreat, stay in touch.

- Reevaluate while conversations and interactions are fresh in your mind.

- During the reevaluate phase, dig deep to ask, "What is going wrong?"

- Take a complete physical inventory of yourself.

- Reapproach and state fault or error.

- Choose graciousness over coercion.

- Ask *why* you lost the business.

- Establish patience as your virtue.

Chapter 13

Let's Revisit a Deal

Remember this your lifetime through:
Tomorrow there will be more to do.
And failure waits for those who stay
With some success made yesterday.
Tomorrow you must try once more,
And even harder than before.

—John Wooden

I t has been said that patience comes to those who wait. Have you ever pitched a deal that you thought your contact was extremely interested in, but when it came time to close the deal, you were told, "Thanks, but no thanks. The timing isn't right." Did you apply the three Rs—retreat, reevaluate, and reapproach—but still not get a commitment? The biggest question of all now, folks, is: Did you *follow up* with that client six months or a year or more later?

Just because a client can't purchase your product or service today does not mean he or she won't buy it tomorrow. By learning to document and track those times your contacts expressed interest but did not buy, you can find a wealth of new business in long-forgotten files and piles.

Got Closer?

Sheryl Leach was a savvy businesswoman and mother. She was frustrated in the late 1980s with the quality of children's programming on television and had taken the initiative to write, direct, and produce her own children's video,

Barney the Dinosaur. Sheryl, who was president of The Lyons Group at the time, wanted to know if I could help her find distribution for her product. She had been able to position the purchase of her video in a test market situation at Toys 'R' Us, but they weren't spending any effort marketing her product. After all, it was a single video, a one-hit wonder. It didn't have any shelf presence mixed in with thousands of other children's videos they carried.

Our firm launched a contest in which our 3,000 field representatives who called on retail accounts had carte blanche to go into grocery stores, drugstores, mass merchandisers, video outlets, neighborhood gift shops—anywhere they could find a warm body—and try to pitch the video. After a year of trying, we had achieved very little success. It was a children's video, and it was only one product. Short of sitting down and watching it, no one we called on could grasp its potential.

Sheryl, however, was not one to take "no" for an answer. She created two more videos and designed a cute plush Barney the Dinosaur stuffed animal. Now we're talking! She had enough products to cause purchasers to sit up and notice. She went back to Toys 'R' Us, and this time, the buyers purchased the full line for all of the Toys 'R' Us stores.

Barney went on to have his own TV show, clothing line, videos, CDs, lunch boxes, and paper towels. Sheryl and Barney became an empire. And Toys 'R' Us? Its buyers couldn't buy enough of Sheryl's products to keep up with the demand in its stores. The moral of this story? Never give up, and always go back. Your contacts from yesterday may become your biggest customers tomorrow.

Let's look at how we can turn some of those "Come back a year from now" situations into "Let's do some business today." The first thing you can do is start tracking your clients, the dates you've contacted them, their reactions, and if and when they asked you to get back to them. What's your reaction when a gig you thought was golden goes to another competitor? Usually the lead falls to the bottom of our pile and is forgotten. Instead, send a letter stating, "Although I am disappointed that your decision went in a different direction, I am very grateful you included me in the evaluation process. I hope you will keep me in mind for future opportunities as they arise for your company. Thank you again for your kind consideration."

Call the client a month after he or she has been using your competitor. Inquire if the client is satisfied and if he or she plans to continue to do business with the other company. Restate your interest. Impress your prospects with your persistence and professionalism. More likely than not, you'll eventually get the sale! Stay close to the deal. You don't want to forget about prospects, but even more important, you don't want to let them forget about *you*.

Ask your prospect, "Is there another way we might start doing business together? I realize that you are using KickStart Marketing for your current projects that we discussed, but perhaps you'll be reevaluating your business plan later this year, and I may still be able to help you."

Another way to reopen the door is to explore other options: Is there another person within that organization who may be a better fit for you and what you have to offer? Have any of the features or benefits of what you are selling changed, been updated, or been improved? Has your company stream-lined its production and can now offer the product or service at a reduced cost?

Sometimes Phones Don't Ring

It's been three days, and you haven't received a single call. Nada. Zip. You start to wonder, "Have I fallen off the face of the Earth?" And then you remember: You haven't placed any calls either.

Quiet can be a good thing. Catch up on your paperwork, do that necessary research, write that article for your trade publication, and catch up on your reading. But most important is this: You can always pick up the phone yourself and revisit every contact. Conversation is a two-way street.

Bird Out of a Close

Just as in life, everything changes. It's up to you to capitalize on those changes, revisit past prospects, and close more deals. Once again, I turn to my friend

Steven Schussler. For years Steven had wanted to build a restaurant based on the tropical rain forest. Having difficulty getting investors interested in his idea, he decided to turn his suburban home into a prototype of the Rainforest Café. His split-level home was transformed into a jungle, complete with 40 tropical birds, two 150-pound tortoises, a baboon, an iguana, and tropical fish in ten 300-gallon tanks. That wasn't enough, though: It also took 3,700 extension cords to fuel the lights, fog pumps, mist, and jungle noises that filled his home.

Steve turned his attention to a particularly savvy Minnesota businessman: Lyle Berman, a gaming executive and venture capitalist. After giving Lyle a tour of his concept, Steve asked Lyle what he thought of it. Lyle told Steve he needed to see a psychiatrist and that there was "no way" he'd ever invest in his crazy idea.

Steve is not one to take "no" for an answer, so he asked Lyle to bring his kids to see the house. After thrilling the kids with his homemade jungle, Lyle once again assured Steve that he had *no* interest in investing but might he bring his parents over, too, to see what Steve had designed?

Over the years, Steve never let Lyle out of his sight. It took two years of revisits, but Lyle finally agreed and helped raise the necessary funds to launch the Rainforest Café. Steven and his public company owned and operated 45 Rainforest Cafés in seven years on three continents and sold the chain to Landry's Restaurants for $85 million.

Steve did a lot of things right. For one, he didn't take the first "no" as the final "no." He kept Perk-O-Lating the deal by allowing Lyle to bring his family and friends to see his wild dream. But the most important thing Steve did was to revisit Lyle every couple of months . . . for years. Steve didn't allow Lyle to drop to the bottom of his investor pile. He kept in touch. And in the end, it paid off big for Steve. It can pay off big for you, too.

Journey Back to Abundance

Tim Sanders, former chief solutions officer for Yahoo!, shot to fame and fortune with his best-selling book *Love Is the Killer App.* It's easy to imagine someone like Tim swimming in abundance, but he didn't start out that way. Tim honed his management skills and techniques running a fireworks stand at the tender age of 12. He learned many lessons running the stand: how to talk fast, think on his feet, count money, and share profits. After all, he hired other kids from trailer parks, farms, and the inner city to help him run his business.

Sure, he learned the value of profit margins, but he learned something bigger: the joy of helping people grow professionally and the joy he took on his journey to abundance. But Tim was only 12; he hadn't experienced scarcity or the heartbreak of the trail or competition.

The years progressed and Tim fell into the rut of corporate America. He was drawn to organizations that were troubled and struggling. Abundance was replaced by fear. Tim describes these early experiences as "scarcity on steroids."

But he learned the biggest lesson of his life during these difficult times. He learned about the Larry Archers of the world.

Larry Archer was a fellow employee at Tim's production company in Dallas. In his mid-50's and with his full white beard, he resembled Santa Claus and acted like him, too. He was wise beyond his position in the company. Larry would eat in the lunchroom every day, and Tim (being ambitious and hungry, too) would join him. Larry taught Tim about discipline and motivation and reminded Tim daily that self-esteem came first.

The company was growing fast and furious, and Tim's days in the lunchroom disappeared. One day, Tim received a sales report notifying him that he had not filled his quota. Remembering the wisdom and humanity of Larry, he decided to turn to him for advice. Tim has never forgotten the words he heard on the other end of the phone: "Tim, you are so out of touch. Larry died a week ago."

Since that moment Tim has been on a mission of atonement: to find the Larry Archers of the world. No one deserves to be forgotten or neglected, and it was only through this hard lesson in life that Tim has come back on his journey to abundance.

Who are your Larry Archers? Call them and tell them that you care. Then call them again just for the heck of it. Dale Carnegie wrote long ago: "You can make more friends in two months by becoming interested in other people than you can in two years trying to get other people interested in you."

Call. *Call often.*

Here's the Real Deal

- Your contacts from yesterday may become your biggest customers tomorrow.
- Track your disappointments.
- Call your prospects a month after they start using the competition.
- Explore other options; ask, "Is there another way we can start doing business together?"
- Conversation is a two-way street.
- Call. *Call often.*

Section V

Here's the Real Deal

Success is to be measured not so much by the position that one has reached in life as by the obstacles which he has overcome while trying to succeed.

—Booker T. Washington

Chapter 14

Let's Follow Up a Deal

You did it! You closed the deal! Now what? You can sit back, relax, and count your chickens—or you can immediately start taking the steps toward turning that one closed deal into a long-term client. We all know the myriad efforts that went into making this sale: the connections we made and the packaging, marketing, and Perk-O-Lating. We don't want to have to start from scratch all over again, do we?

Learning to thank your customers in spectacular ways that are memorable and life-lasting is a major step toward creating loyals for life. Loyals for life are those customers who set up a chain of business that perpetuates year after year. Word-of-mouth referrals come from satisfied and loyal customers. Let's look at an example of how to thank people for their business.

> *There are two types of people—those who come into a room and say,*
> *"Well, here I am," and those who come in and say, "Ah, there you are."*
>
> —Frederick Collins

Frequent Closer

Over the course of a year, I had one of the *best* and one of the *worst* years of my life.

In January of that year, I closed the biggest deal of my sales career: a multimillion-dollar contract with Procter & Gamble (P&G) that literally doubled the size of our company overnight. P&G had been an active and large account for me at SPAR Marketing Services, with our company providing their retail service support (putting up point-of-purchase materials, cutting new products into retail space, audits, surveys, etc.) in outlets such as Kmart, Target, Lowe's, Bradlees, and a number of retailers who have long since gone out of business.

P&G had discovered that, over the years, they had 20 different service company providers, and they wanted to consolidate. I was fairly confident we'd at least be in the final evaluations because I had done all the things I've written about in this book, including providing exceptional customer service. I had an excellent relationship with several of their key account managers.

In the elimination process, four companies were left standing. It was now time to whittle that down to two. Site visits were scheduled to meet the players involved with each company, tour their facilities, confirm their commitment to take on such an enormous project, and review our proposals.

The day for our site visit, I walked the entire office looking for every small detail. I replaced anyone's facial tissues that weren't P&G's with a new box of Puffs. I put Bounty paper towels in our break room and Joy detergent on the kitchen sink. We made the "Welcome Procter & Gamble" sign with everyone's name listed and put it in our lobby. We were all ready for inspection.

That day at noon I picked up my main contact, Bruce, and three others at the airport. Thinking I'd take them to the fanciest restaurant in town, I had made reservations at a place where I thought I could close the deal. But when we got in the car, I remembered my golden rule: Don't forget to ask!

"Gentlemen, is there any place in particular you'd like to go for lunch?" I inquired.

Bruce said, "Christine, I ate at this little deli once in Minneapolis. They had a sandwich I've never forgotten. It was made out of hamburger, but cheese and pimentos were cooked right into the meat. Does that ring a bell? It was one of the best sandwiches I've ever eaten."

"Why, that would be the Lincoln Del, Bruce, and the sandwich is called The Delwich. It's one of my favorites, too, and it's right on the way to the office. Let's go!"

We ate at the Lincoln Del that day, and afterward, the men stopped by our office. They walked in and out in less than an hour, and I drove them back to the airport. And then I waited . . .

I was still sleeping that morning when my phone rang at 6:30 AM. "Christine, this is Bruce. I've got good news and bad news. Which would you like first?"

Groggily I said, "Well, give me the good news first!"

"The good news is that you got the Procter & Gamble business, Christine!"

"Well, that's incredible news, Bruce! Thank you so much! What could possibly be the bad news?"

"You got the Procter & Gamble business, Christine. Your life will never be the same," said Bruce as he chuckled, knowing P&G's reputation as a demanding client.

I asked Bruce what we had done to secure his business that the others hadn't done.

"Besides the fact that we've been working with you for years now, Christine, it was your willingness to take us to the Lincoln Del!" he teased. "But no, seriously, when we walked into your offices, we just felt comfortable. You and the rest of the employees at SPAR seemed like an extension of our company. We look forward to many years of service together."

The business came with a price. I spent more than 250 nights on the road that year, putting out fires and trying to meet all of the P&G managers around the country. As the year was coming to an end, I couldn't wait to get home for the holidays to reconnect with my family and friends and maybe even (gasp) spend some time relaxing.

My plans for a restful holiday were not to be. On December 19 I was diagnosed with breast cancer, and my doctor recommended I have surgery almost immediately. Two weeks later, on New Year's Eve, I went into the hospital for the operation. Thankfully, it went without complications. When I returned from the hospital, I walked into my home office and surveyed two mountains of mail that had been accumulating all year long. My boys had made a game out of who could build the highest stack, and, truthfully, it looked insurmountable. I waded through it in the days following my surgery, moved by the many cards from associates and friends wishing me a speedy recovery.

Two business-related letters in that stack demonstrated for me the choice we have to either continue a deal or cancel a deal. One was from Northwest Airlines and the other was from a major hotel chain that shall remain nameless. The purpose of their letters was to notify me that, "Congratulations! You have achieved Platinum status for the upcoming year in our Frequent Guest Programs."

As those of you who travel a lot know, those Platinum programs have a lot of Perk-O-Lating going on and make business travel a lot more comfortable and easy. I knew it would be a while before I was back out on the road due to my upcoming treatment schedule, which meant I wouldn't be in a position to take advantage of these programs for months, if not the entire year. So, I wrote a letter to the two organizations explaining my circumstances and asking if they would please consider deferring my Platinum status to the following year. Three weeks went by, and I got a form letter from the hotel chain:

Dear Christine:

We received your request. While we regret to learn that this has happened to you, "things" happen to people: they lose their jobs, they get divorced, they move, they pass away. We're sorry, but we are unable to defer your Platinum status with us. We hope to see you soon.

About a week later, I got a handwritten letter from John Dasburg, the president of Northwest Airlines himself. It read:

Dear Christine, How can we begin to thank you for being one of our very best customers? We will not only defer your Platinum status for one year, but enclosed please find four complimentary airline tickets to take you and your family away from the cold Minnesota winter and give you a break from your treatments.

Thank you, Christine, for your business. Good luck. We'll miss you this year.

You can imagine my different reactions to the two different letters. Do you want to know the irony in all of this? For any of you who may have flown through the Minneapolis/St. Paul area, you know that Northwest (now Delta) owns the majority of the 117 gates in our airport—including all of Terminal G—because they were once headquartered there and were headquartered there when this story took place. Northwest could have easily told me, "Christine, *things* happen to people. We can't accommodate your request," and I still would have had to fly Northwest because, back then, there wasn't much of a choice.

But I can stand here today and proudly tell you that I am a loyal Northwest/Delta customer *by choice,* and I will be a Northwest/Delta customer *for life.* I have never again stayed in that hotel chain.

The chief executive officer (CEO) of Northwest/Delta went out of his way to acknowledge my patronage of his company's services and reached out to me as a person, not just as a customer. That type of above and beyond the call service is so rare, it engenders passionate loyalty in return.

How can you thank your customers in spectacular ways that are memorable and life-lasting? How can you reach out to them and let them know you genuinely value their patronage? How can you follow up and go above and beyond in an extraordinary fashion that rewards and perpetuates their loyalty? Find out how because, believe me—it will be worth the effort.

You can always purchase a copy of Robyn Freedman Spizman's book *The Thank You Book: Hundreds of Clever, Meaningful and Purposeful Ways to Say Thank You,* or here are a few suggestions.

Clever Ways to Say "Thank You!"

- Anything custom-made or personalized—from a thank-you note, to chocolates (M&M's are always fun), to an engraved desk calendar, to an autographed photo of one of their idols—is always a hit and shows "I took the time to have this made for you."

- Hire a local bakery to make fresh cookies or cupcakes and have them delivered while they are still fresh and warm out of the oven.

- Spend time looking around their office or home, if you've had the privilege, to see if there is something the person collects. Finding a "one of a kind" for someone's collection of glass frogs shows you are paying attention.

- Tickets to sporting events, the theater, or concerts are always appropriate, but make it even more special by arranging to have the person taken backstage or on the field.

- Anything homemade—from meals to candy to candles to soap—is always a great gesture and deeply appreciated.

- Have a video made of your client's customers expressing how much they appreciate the company.

- Send a crew to the client's office with all the ingredients to make ice cream sundaes.

- Present a U.S. flag that has flown over the capitol. Call your congressman or congresswoman's office to order one.

From the smallest gesture of a handwritten note, to sending a cookie bouquet by Cookies for Design, to sending a hand-painted coconut with the words "Go Nuts! Thanks for your business!" (and yes, the U.S. Postal Service will mail coconuts), *any* type of thank you says, "I am so grateful for your business. Your business is important to me. I plan to work with you for a very long time. *Thank you.*"

Fore Close!

Now, as the late renowned radio broadcaster Paul Harvey would have said, "for the rest of the story." I took those four airline tickets given to me by

John Dasburg and Northwest and flew off with my family to Scottsdale, Arizona, when I was halfway through my treatments. While we were there, there was an event being played on the Senior PGA Golf Tour (now the Champions Tour) called the Tradition. We bought tickets to it. This was just what the doctor (and Mr. Dasburg) had prescribed to lift my spirits and give us a fun family outing.

The first day of the tournament brought out a huge gallery. It was a beautiful day, and I was in heaven. I was standing just off the third tee, behind the fairway ropes, watching three of my favorite golfers approach the tee box: Jack Nicklaus, Raymond Floyd, and Tom Weiskopf.

Just as they arrived at the tee, the unimaginable happened. A huge gust of wind came up from out of nowhere and blew my hat *and* my hair right off my head and right into the middle of the fairway! The thousands of spectators lining the fairway fell into an awkward silence, all eyes on me. There wasn't a peep! Even my golf idols were watching me, seeing as my wig was in their flight path. I was mortified. Embarrassed as I was, I knew I couldn't just stand there. Someone had to do something to get things moving again.

So I took a deep breath, went under the ropes, and ran out into the middle of the fairway. I grabbed my hat and my hair and nestled them back on my head as best I could. Then I turned to the golfers and loudly announced, "Gentlemen, the wind is blowing from left to right!"

Who knows how those lines occurred to me? Wherever they came from, I was grateful because they say the laughter could be heard all the way to the nineteenth hole. As the golfers teed off and headed down the fairway, I slipped incognito back into the crowd. With my wig and hat firmly placed on my head, no one could tell that I was the bald lady who moments ago wanted to die from embarrassment. But something else happened that day. As we made our way around the golf course, I could hear people retelling the story to complete strangers, and they'd all laugh wholeheartedly at what had transpired. Don't forget to laugh!

Why have I shared this embarrassing moment with you? Because it demonstrates how we can rescue a deal when it goes south. We can follow up what looks like a disaster with quick-on-our-feet recovery that saves the day—and the deal. Let's summarize what happened here:

1. Northwest realized that I was a loyal for life and wanted to thank me for my business in a spectacular way that was memorable and life-lasting.

2. Just as in sales, the unimaginable happened. I could have panicked and reacted with horror, or I could think on my feet and come up with a comeback. I didn't let that get the best of me.

3. I realized that I had to take control of the awkward situation. Just as in the pitch and present, sometimes we are the ones who have to keep the ball in forward motion. It was up to me to turn this situation around. I couldn't wait to be rescued.

4. I followed the three Rs—retreat, reevaluate, and reapproach—albeit in an accelerated version pulled off in seconds. By bringing humor into the equation, I was able to turn what could have been a disaster into an indelible memory.

We never know which way the wind is going to blow in our careers. We can let it knock us off balance, or we can adjust our sails, put out our spinnaker, and have the wind at our back propelling us along. If your deal is about to go sour, can you think fast to adapt to the changing circumstances? Can you follow up with dissatisfied customers in a way that brings them back into the fold? Can you demonstrate loyalty to them in their difficult times so they'll choose to stick with you over time?

Our sales opportunities can change on a dime. But every change brings with it something new, unexpected, and exciting. So how can you create loyals for life—customers who will be with you for years and years and will refer new clients to you?

I've found that clients, like friends, come and go. But there are a lot of similarities in how you treat—and like to be treated—by both. I put this question out to some of my loyals for life. Here are their responses:

I believe people come into your life for a reason; some remain life-long friends and clients, and others are a gift to provide short-term insight to a problem and to lend support and love during a specifically difficult time. My lifelong relationships have sustained when there is a shared commonality of values, beliefs, interests, and deep commitment. Long-term relationships require nurturing, thoughtfulness, and caring.

Why some people remain in your heart forever and some for a short time is a mystery, but when realized becomes a true gift from God.

—Margie Sborov, Founder, Angel Foundation

I have found through my businesses that my Loyals for Life are clients with whom I have developed a personal relationship by finding out more about them and their lives. Often, the relationship started by me helping them via my products (jewelry) or services (GoldSwap) and they learned that they could rely on me and trust me so they continue to come back to me and refer their family and friends to me.

—Kim Julen, Host, GoldSwap

Overpromise, then overdeliver. In other words, provide a Wow! experience right away. In my consulting business, I promise a 10-fold return on their investment return (typical in my industry is 2–4 fold), and then I strive to actually give them a 20-fold return.

After that, there are other tactics for retaining those clients. First, you have your main product or service with which you made the Wow! impression. But then have back-end products and services for them to choose from also. Second, you might have a product or service that you can offer on a "subscription" basis. Finally, in order to ensure that you always deliver high value, take these steps: a) show them you care; b) create a good first impression; c) handle complaints promptly and generously; d) continuously survey your customers to see what they want, what they like, and how they feel about your product or service.

—Rick Swanson, CEO/President, Learning Meets Quality LLC

For me it comes down to understanding and meeting each other where you're at throughout life's stages.

I recently lost a friendship because we are in different stages of life. My friend doesn't have children and many of the other demands that exist in my life. While we connected on a deep level, trusted each other, and had fun, she had expectations (or standards of how she wanted to be treated) that weren't realistic for me. I could show up in a way that met her needs some of the time (quick response communication, making plans far in advance, etc.) but not consistently. Although I was hurt and disappointed in her abrupt decision to step away from our friendship, I realized it was a positive for me, a release from underlying pressure and inflexibility.

The relationships I know will stand the test of time ebb and flow with the stages in life. When my kids are grown I know my ability to participate socially and be more involved in the community will change. Much of this has to do with the number of hours in a day and priorities. My priorities today are my children, job, and recovery. It doesn't mean there aren't more pieces to the pie (chart), they are simply smaller sections right now today. We don't get TWO pies either!!!

—Alison Nelson, Community Relations Manager, Tubman

My tip for you is: authenticity. I have been with Arbonne for 20+ years and have clients who have been with me for 18 years!!

—Barbara Moser, Independent Consultant, Executive
National Vice President, ARBONNE

Whether it be a personal or business relationship, my focus is on a heartfelt centered approach. In other words, I strive to relate to others on an emotional level. It is my belief that great opportunities arise from great connections. Many of my business relationships convert into friendships for life.

Being an aggressive, conniving, or a deceitful salesperson doesn't play into my matrix. Being open, honest, trustworthy, and compassionate does. By relating to others I am able to find a positive outcome when it comes to someone's issues/situation. Compassion goes a long way in building loyalty. I don't always know how things will work out so I try not to get stuck on "how." Instead I take action and quite often get what I request by knowing what is in my "power" to do.

—Linda Margl, Certified Real Estate Expert,
Edina Realty

Just because you don't hear from your clients doesn't mean that they are happy. Stay in touch . . . and stay in touch often. Be proactive.

—Robert Grant, Vice President—Investments,
Wells Fargo Advisors, LLC

Because I know me from the inside out and what I value in myself and the services I provide, I am very clear about who I want to work with and why. I connect with clients on a deep personal level because I can solve their problems. Asking for help for many is a sign of weakness. I reframe that to be a sign of strength, courage, and willingness to grow out of the comfort zone to the fabulous yet uncertain uncomfort zone.

Because I love my clients, I tell them that and show that to them. They feel safe. Safe and loved = loyal. I am their board of directors to whom they can go with most things they cannot confide to others. Strict confidentiality. And because I love them, I go out of my way to give extras such as availability for 911 (calls like I make to you, Christine!) which is rarely used because they trust themselves to know what is 911 and [what is] not. I tailor their experiences and provide them additional support beyond the coaching contract.

Loyalty = Love = Living with my clients through the thick and thin of business and life and never giving up on them, even though they feel like giving up on themselves, and always holding them to their bigger self.

—Mary Schmid, Life Coach,
Business CPR

When someone is experiencing a challenging time, don't ask what you could do for them; listen to Nike, and "Just do it!" When a friend or client is going through a hard time, I don't ask, "If you need anything, call me." I initiate something, from bringing them a meal to cutting their lawn. People feel awkward asking for help; you remove this uncomfortable feeling by just doing something.

People don't forget these acts of kindness and that is why they stay in your life.

—Edward Leigh, MA, Founder & Director, Center for Healthcare Communication

Here's my tip to establish lifelong professional and personal relationships: The dying art of making a phone call.

In today's world, email and texting seem to be the "way to go" because it is believed to be easier and more efficient. But that is not always true. As a group sales manager at a theater, I prefer to make phone calls to our clients and many are surprised to be able to speak with a real person. In a world of online booking and automated computer assistants, sometimes just hearing a real person's voice on the other line makes a client feel like they are receiving more personalized service.

In my personal life, I prefer to call my friends when I need to communicate with them because that opens the door for more genuine conversation—if the other person is willing. In addition to discussing the topic at hand, a door is opened for free-flowing conversation for us to talk about our lives in more meaningful ways. I can often hear a friend's emotions through their speech, and lend a listening ear if they are troubled, or celebrate with them if they are joyful. And the same is true for clients.

—Deb Sand, Group Manager, Jungle Theater Group

Real relationships require being "open and honest." I've always just been me. Have a conversation and don't worry about the "Sale."

Do what's right for your client. Help first . . . there's something in the karma that brings people back over and over.

—CJ DuBé, Certified EOS Implementer, Achieve Traction

I have noticed that when I show an interest in a client's personal life as well as in them professionally, and I remember the names of their family members and ask about them, they respond. I am actually interested in them in and it is genuine and they sense that.

—Susan Jacobs, Owner, Casa Verde Design

Every one of my customers has a story, literally. I listen and offer solutions as an outsider if you will. Sometimes it's easier to talk with people you don't know just for an outside perspective. I consider myself open and live by the philosophy that there are three sides to every story! With all of my EXperience, I truly believe my customers really listen to me and want to share their stories.

—Beth Price, Owner, Divorce Shower Store

I treat my clients like I treat my lifelong best friend, Carla Mitchum, who lives where I grew up—in Ozark, Missouri. I gave her a birthday gift a couple of months ago: a collage of three pictures. The first was taken when we were 15; the second when we were about 25; and the third from when we were 44 I think. The inscription read: "31 years; 627.48 miles; Still Best Friends Forever." We never let too many days go by without calling, emailing or texting. Several years ago we started picking a vacation destination and meet there with our kids. Last summer she made me go parasailing in Florida! I go "home" to visit about three times a year, and always stay at her house. She comes up once about every other year. When I'm on her front porch it's like we were never 600 miles apart. When my grandma was in a nursing home, I went down every two to six weeks for three years. She gave me a bed to sleep in every time, and always had my favorite pop in the fridge. She is and always will be my very best friend, no matter how many years pass or how many miles away we are. We both know that we are just one phone call and 10 hours at most away if the other one needs her. Unconditional love, always *on each other's side, and behind each other 100%, no matter what!*

—Holly Zelinsky, President, Nationally Speaking, Inc.

Acknowledge them with a memorable card or gift to let them know you are always thinking about them.

—Dawn Stebbing, Certified Image Consultant, CEO/ President, Image Evolution, Inc.

Send them something inexpensive (a desk calendar, a bookmark, a notepad, a PC screen duster, etc.) at Christmas time, or some other holiday, with a personal note.

—Adaire Lassonde, Program Specialist, Catholic Charities

"Golden Rule" always seems to answer most issues I have as to how to treat somebody in a given situation. I ask myself, "How would I like to be treated?" Simple, but good basic guidance.

—Parrel Caplan, Attorney, Founder/CEO, The Wow Bar, Blow Dry & Style Bar

Learn and keep up to date with the personal details of a client's or referral source's life. Know their kids' names and where they go to college, or what their prior job was and where they grew up. It shows you care. Also help refer them to another resource that they

need; help them in some way that doesn't directly benefit you. They will remember the good gesture.

—Cathy E. Gorlin, Attorney, Best & Flanagan

I remain loyal to my hair salon. They are more expensive than any other salon I've been to but I get more than a great service, I get an "experience." Juut on Grand Ave in St. Paul, MN makes sure that every step along the way is peaceful and indulgent. They take your coat, offer you a beverage, seat you in a cozy area with plenty of the most expensive women's magazines, start your session with a head massage of yummy scented essential oils, walk you to the product center to personally assist you (sales brilliance) and escort you to check out. And, they always ask to book your next appointment.

I remain loyal for three reasons:

- *Excellent product or service*
- *Good value or competitive price*
- *All the people I deal with are nice (Beware of the rude frontline employee, he or she can ruin a relationship in an instant).*

—Molly Cox, President, StrongCoffeeink

I have clients who have been extremely loyal to me through two different businesses as well as a re-brand for one of the businesses. Some reasons for the loyalty:

- *They fit within the demographic of my ideal target market (woman, passionate about their businesses, positive attitude, authentic, uplifting) so the services I've offered have been precisely the right fit for their needs.*

- *I operate with a mission-driven mind-set in running business. The overall mission is to nurture and create opportunities for women to lift each other up for business success. Many of the women we serve feel strongly about the overall mission and want to support it by being involved, registering for our events, becoming members.*

- *Consistency/authenticity in the brand: The clients who are so loyal appreciate that they know they will receive care and quality when they participate in something I offer through the services I provide.*

- *I pay attention to details about them so that I can customize their experience and reflect back to them how important they are to me.*

—**Teresa Thomas, Director, Women In Networking (WIN)**

I have been in sales for more than 30 years. I have never tried to sell anything to anyone. Each day I wake up to the greatest gift in my life: I get to meet new people and learn all about them. As an auctioneer, my job is to discover what people want to sell, learn the story behind the items, and in the course of the conversation, I learn a lot about the person and many times about their family. Everyone has a story, and if you let them speak, they are happy to share it. The "sale" just happens because you have become a friendly face, a good listener, and someone who genuinely knows and cares about their story."

—**Michelle A. Williams, Owner,
M.A. Williams Auctions and Appraisals**

Do you see a pattern starting to emerge? Clients—like friends—want to be nurtured, cared for, and made to feel important. By making the transition from salesmanship to friendship, you, too, can create loyals for life.

How do you generate referrals and word-of-mouth business from your loyals for life? The most important thing you can do is to ask for referrals. "Adam, you've told me how happy you've been with the work I've been doing for you. Do you, by any chance, have one or two friends or clients of your own who you feel may also benefit from my services? I would be extremely grateful to you for any referrals you can give me."

Give clients extra copies of your business cards or brochures. Ask them if they'll post something positive about you on your LinkedIn account or Facebook page. Have them talk about you on Twitter.

If one of your existing clients gives you a referral, thank him or her in a spectacular way that is memorable and life-lasting. Keep the circle of friendship moving.

Here's the Real Deal

- Thank your customers in spectacular ways that are memorable and life-lasting to create loyals for life.
- Ask your clients, "What would you love?"
- Create clever ways to say "thank you."
- Follow up: Rescue a deal when it goes south with quick-on-your-feet recoveries.
- Ask for referrals.

Chapter 15

Let's Revel in a Deal

It is not easy to find happiness in ourselves,
And it is not possible to find it elsewhere.

—Agnes Repplier

W hen is the last time you threw yourself a celebration for the successes you've had in your career? Do you take the time or make the time to pat yourself on the back? Selling as a career can be a very lonely life. Some of us are traveling sales professionals, spending countless hours on the road by ourselves. Some of us work out of home offices where the only one to congratulate us at the end of the day is the family dog. Others are entrepreneurial "one-man/woman bands" with rental space in strip malls and contract help for secretarial services.

Whether you work alone or for a major corporation, reveling in your deals is your right and reward for your hard labor. I also believe it is your *responsibility* to take the time to reflect and appreciate all that you've accomplished. If you skip over this final step of closing a deal, it becomes hard work instead of a joyous, satisfying process.

It is easier to go down a hill than up,
But the view is from the top.

—Anonymous

On the recommendation of a mutual friend, I met a total stranger for a cup of coffee on April 22, 2010. We had actually met at a networking meeting a few months earlier when I had spoken at the event, and she came up to my book-signing table afterward. "Christine," she said, "we need to get together. I'm an author, too, and I think we have a lot in common."

While I'm all about making connections and following up on leads, my schedule was swamped, and truthfully, I kind of blew her off. But Barb Greenberg wasn't going to take "no" for an answer. A few days after the event, she left me a voice mail. It was so long I didn't even listen to the entire message. When I didn't respond, an e-mail came. I jotted something back to her quickly, hoping she might lose interest. But then Barb did what I have recommended you do: She Perk-O-Lated our getting together by spending money to make money. Barb sent me a copy of her wonderful book, *After the Ball: A Woman's Tale of Reclaiming Happily Ever After.*

Sitting together in a window seat in a Caribou Coffee shop a few days later, we shared stories of our divorces. I came to realize how challenging this experience is for most people: Where do I start? Who do I speak with? Where do I turn for help? How am I going to survive? What about the kids? There were so many questions.

I also realized that I was approaching my divorce from a position of power: I was the one who filed for divorce. But Barb, who had been blindsided after a 33-year marriage, said she could hardly get out of bed in the morning. And it occurred to me: What about all the people who feel as though their lives have come to an end? Can we provide the tools to help them feel like they can move forward?

During our 2-hour meeting we came up with the concept of our company, Divorcing Divas: a company to provide encouragement, inspiration, and empowerment to people going through the difficult process of divorce. Through support, education, resources, and hope, we would show divorcees that they can find life—and a *good* life—on the other side.

But that's not all we did in that first meeting: On paper napkins we wrote our slogan, tagline, and mission statement; jotted down an agenda for our first all-day educational conference; chose a date; and had a list of potential speakers. The only problem? Because of our divorces, we had no money!

Barb Greenberg and I were so convinced that we were on to something that we took a huge risk: We both committed to invest $2,000 in our start-up. I immediately went home and purchased the URL that day, contacted my patent attorney (yes, it was available!), and started soliciting website designers. Next I asked my recent college graduate son Brooks if he would be willing to design a logo for us . . . free of charge. He said he was definitely up to the challenge—it was the least he could do in exchange for the college education he had received.

We went to our bank, Wells Fargo, and opened a business checking account with our $4,000 investment. Barb started interviewing hotels to host our venue (not free!). We had to sign a contract guaranteeing at least $8,000 in revenue.

Together, the two of us started calling individuals who would have the content we were looking for as speakers and presenters—financial planning, the legal journey, emotional support, well-being, and even humor—but also be willing to speak . . . for free!

The wheels were in motion. But we quickly made our first big mistake: We hired the wrong guy to design our website. In fact, we broke my cardinal rule: It takes money to make money. Not having much money, we first went with the low-cost provider. Our needs were out of his league: online registration, a shopping cart, and a content management system. We lost almost three weeks trying to find another.

We hired a midlevel designer to do the work on our site. Time was running out. We only had four months until our first event, and now we were under contract with the hotel. He took more than two months to design the site after telling us he could do it in two weeks! We were now down to two months to market and sell tickets to the event.

We officially launched our company on June 21, 2010, and as soon as the website was up and operational, I started contacting the media with a press release I wrote myself. My good friend Jean Golden, who is a public relations expert, took a look at it and made suggestions. Success! The media was fascinated by our concept. I secured two appearances on our local NBC affiliate and was interviewed in several print publications, including the two major newspapers in the Twin Cities.

Five months from that fateful day in the coffee shop, on September 25, we held our first event titled Happily Ever After. We sold sponsorships and vendor tables, selling out within three weeks. And we charged a fee per person to attend the all-day event.

The result? More than 200 people attended that conference. Barb and I paid ourselves back for our full investment and made a small profit. We made a generous donation to our nonprofit partner Tubman (www.Tubman.org), a women's shelter for abused women in the Twin Cities. And we invested in having our event filmed so we could have a powerful video clip to show the potential sponsors and vendors for our next event, which was held less than five months later on February 12, 2011, and titled Be Your Own Valentine!

But the greatest gift of all came as a comment on one of our evaluation forms from the first event. It read, "When I arrived at your conference, I was petrified with fear. I am leaving today knowing that your event saved my life."

Sometimes our celebrations can be as simple as words. We've made a difference, helped someone, or changed someone's life. It doesn't get any better than that.

Sometimes opportunities are where you never expected to find them. I didn't want to meet Barb that day for coffee; I had too much to do. But two heads are better than one, and in a moment's time, we launched a successful new business.

After a few years, Barb decided to leave the business to devote time to her grandchildren, her writing, and her small divorce consulting business, Happily Ever After. Today, I have an active committee of 11 who manage everything from vendor tables to in-kind donations (for door prizes, raffle items, and live auction items to raise money for Tubman) to passing out event fliers and postcards. We have strong partnerships with sponsors, a printing company, a new webmaster, graphic designers, and vendors.

We've used social media to attract everything from committee members to attendees to vendors and sponsors with services on Twitter, Facebook,

Meetup, and LinkedIn. And we send out press releases and story ideas to media contacts both locally and nationally on a daily basis.

We increased our visibility for our events by securing one of our celebrity news anchors from NBC to serve as our honorary emcee for the day. We submitted and were approved for continuing education credits from the Minnesota Boards of Psychology, Social Workers, and Nursing. We believe this adds tremendous credibility to the content we are presenting at our conference.

What did we do right? We never stopped believing in ourselves. If you believe in yourself, your product, your service, your company, or your cause, anything is possible. It's not the end . . . it's the beginning.

Don't feel entitled to anything you didn't sweat and struggle for.

—**Marian Wright Edelman, President of the Children's Defense Fund**

What should you do when you've closed a big deal, sold your company, or watched your profits soar? HUG yourself. *HUG* acknowledges that you are a "highly unique genius." You really do need to embrace all that you've accomplished. No one else could have done what you did. Another might have achieved some type of success, but it wouldn't have been the way *you* did it.

Climb Every Mountain, Close Every Deal

I mentioned earlier in the book about having an opportunity to speak in Munich for a multinational company. I had been missing time with my family due to my heavy travel schedule, so I decided to reward myself by bringing my youngest son Brooks with me. Brooks had been studying German for three years, and I thought it would be a perfect opportunity for him to utilize his learning and for me to spend precious time alone with one of my kids.

When the sales meeting was over and I had said my "thank yous" and "good-byes" to each attendee and my host, Brooks and I rented a car and drove from Munich to Austria. It was a glorious day, and we zoomed along the autobahn. I was reflecting on the past few days of business and couldn't help but feel a sense of pride about how well the program had gone and was mentally reveling in the standing ovation the group had given me at the end of my presentation.

Austria was everything we had ever imagined. We purchased tickets to take the *Sound of Music* tour right outside of Salzburg, and memories of watching that movie with my family when I was Brooks's age came flooding back.

Part of that tour included going to Mount Dürnberg. Remember the mountaintop where Julie Andrews spread her arms wide and sang, "The hills are alive"? As Brooks and I reached the pinnacle of that extraordinarily beautiful place, I reflected on the past few years. Only eight years earlier, I was in the midst of being diagnosed and treated for cancer. During that frightening time, I wasn't even sure if I would see Brooks graduate from high school. Now, here we were, climbing every mountain together and fording every stream. I was so grateful for this second chance at life. So grateful to be there reveling in that exquisite moment with my son.

I realized then that my entire life has been a win-win-win. Sometimes it's the hardest battles we face, whether in work or in life, that bring us our greatest satisfaction. Brooks may never understand why I had tears running down my face as we viewed the spectacular scenery. But I will always know that for that moment in time, I felt enormous gratitude and a sense of accomplishment. I'd done it. I'd dedicated my life to becoming the best I could be. And nothing could erase that, ever. That realization gave me the strength, encouragement, and validation I needed to continue giving me energy and enthusiasm for everything I do every day.

The Surprise Close

AT&T was one of my biggest and most faithful clients. The national account managers for Kmart, Target, and a dozen other retailers were my direct contacts. But being a shrewd businesswoman, I asked one of my contacts if he would invite Ed May, AT&T's vice president of sales, to join us for dinner the next time I called on them in Parsippany, New Jersey.

The day came, and after a successful meeting, we headed to an exquisite and intimate spot for dinner. It was a rowdy group, and being old friends after so many years of service, a good time was had by all.

The bill came, and I immediately grabbed it and passed my credit card to the waiter. Ed May looked at me in total shock and disbelief. The thought crossed my mind, "What can possibly be wrong here? I invited *him* out to dinner."

And then Ed spoke. "Christine, in all my years of working with AT&T, I have never, and I repeat *never,* had a client, large or small, even *attempt* to pay a bill when AT&T was involved. I've never understood why, but I guess it's because we're so big everyone thinks we're swimming in money. Thank you for restoring my faith in humanity. It's been a great evening and will be one I will never forget."

Surprise your clients; sometimes the right thing to do isn't always done. Celebrate your successes with them. After all, they are the ones who have gotten you here in the first place. Even elephants never forget.

It's my sincerest hope that this book helps you be the best you can be. I hope you have come to realize over the course of the book that closing a deal isn't just something we do on the job. All day, every day we are interacting with others. The way we treat people (all people—not just prospective customers and current clients); the way we communicate with them; and the way we present our ideas, products, and services determines whether they choose to say "yea" or "nay."

I hope you've seen that these suggestions are integrity-based. It is never okay to close a deal that is only self-serving. Not only is it unethical, but it also will come back to haunt you because the best deals serve everyone involved, not just one party. I hope you follow up and use these ideas at work, at home, and in your community and that they help you get more of what you want, need, and deserve—and that in the process, you help others get more of what they want, need, and deserve, too.

Here's the Real Deal

- Reveling in your deals is your right and reward for your hard labor.

- Celebration can be as simple as words.

- If you believe in yourself, your company, your product, your service, or your cause, anything is possible.

- HUG yourself.

- Sometimes the hardest battles you face bring you your greatest satisfaction.

On to the Next Deal

Ask, and it shall be given to you;
seek and ye shall find;
knock and it shall be opened unto you.
For every one that asketh, receiveth;
and he that seeketh, findeth;
and to him that knocketh
it shall be opened.

—Matthew 7:7-8

M y hope is that I've inspired you to take the tools, instructions, and examples found in this book and apply them to your own deals. If we modified the above scripture and applied it to closing a deal, it might read:

- Ask—in compelling ways—and their attention shall be given to you.

- Seek your targeted customers where they like to hang out, and you shall find them.

- Knock on the door of opportunity by finding out what people need—and they shall open the door to doing business with you.

- Fulfill these steps to closing a deal—and you can enrich your personal and professional relationships with win-win-win deals that benefit everyone involved.

Comparing Yourself to Others

Don't. It does you no good to be jealous or envious of what others have achieved. Negative self-talk does nothing for your self-esteem and, in fact, usually makes it worse.

Focus on the positives. We all have them. Then know that if there's something you don't like—about your business, lack of business, appearance, place that you live, place that you don't—you have the ability to change it.

Every day: Focus on the positives.

Old Close

It's human nature to reflect on our lives and our careers and wonder what types of things we might have changed if given the opportunity. But even if I could turn back the hands of time, there are five basic things I have done throughout my varied careers as a top sales producer, marketer, professional speaker, author, and business owner that have propelled me—and the companies I've worked with—to the top of the field, regardless of what type of industry I have been working in.

1. **My focus to create connections that can help me drive my business.** I didn't get where I am today by myself. I've had a lot of people there for me, and with me, every step of the way.

2. **My ability to turn those connections into loyals for life.** I haven't had to waste a lot of valuable time looking for new clients because my loyal clients have sustained me all these years. I have been very blessed in this regard.

3. **The gift I developed over time of learning to spin my ideas into action.** I never took the first "no" as a final "no." If someone didn't like an idea I had or turned me down, I found alternative ways to present it and never let go of my dream.

4. **My desire to be mindful of others and to treat people the way I would like to be treated.** You can almost anticipate when it's about to happen: Someone, totally oblivious of you, commits one of your pet peeves. You're in the aisle seat on an airplane, and an oncoming passenger smashes you—and everyone in his path—in the shoulder with his oversized carry-on. It's 4:30 AM, and you're sleeping in a hotel room. You're rudely awakened by two guys out in the hall talking so loudly about what time they need to get up that morning, having obviously been out all night, that they might as well announce it to the entire building. You've been waiting in line for 20 minutes with dozens of other patient people when someone walks up to the front of the line as if she owns the place. You know the drill. Think of all the things that drive you crazy about others. Then do the opposite. Don't become someone else's pet peeve.

5. **My determination to close every deal.** This is the most important.

How can you accomplish these things? In five easy steps:

1. Always exceed your clients' expectations.
2. With unbridled enthusiasm, get people so pumped up about what it is you do, what it is you sell, or what service you provide, that they can't help but want to get involved with your business.
3. Don't be afraid to ask people for help.
4. Always thank your customers in spectacular ways that are memorable and life-lasting.
5. Don't forget to laugh!

Life gives us one good reason to laugh every chance we get: No one, after all, gets out of here alive. There is a term for the attitude of those who live vitally, with passion and humor: *élan.* It's utterly compelling to others. Italians bestow special praise on people who ignore the weight of life's burdens and live with its lightness. They call that quality *sprezzatura,* which translates not quite perfectly into English as nonchalance. In his famous self-help book of the Renaissance, *The Book of the Courtier,* Castiglione contended that *sprezzatura* is the signal trait of successful people—in his case, the person able to win favor of the members of the Royal Court.

If you are not having fun—if you are not laughing with your clients and your coworkers and yourself—you're in the wrong trade or position. Work *should* be fun. Selling is fun. I hope your approach to the world of closing deals will never be the same and that you will find yourself laughing all the way to retirement. Today is a great day to close a deal!

Thank you.

About the Author

H er experience taught her how to market and sell products, services, and herself. Now, Christine Clifford shares that message with others. Christine Clifford definitely cracked the glass ceiling. By age 40 she was Senior Executive Vice President for The SPAR Group, an international merchandising and information services firm in New York.

As the top salesperson in the multibillion-dollar retail services industry for more than eight years, Christine's accounts included Kmart, Toys 'R' Us, Target, AT&T, Mattel Toys, and Revlon. Taking her company from a million dollar per year loss to more than $54 million in sales, Christine signed the largest contract in the industry's history with Procter & Gamble, doubling the size of her company overnight.

Diagnosed with breast cancer in 1994, Christine wrote eight award-winning, humorous portrayals of her story in books titled *Not Now . . . I'm Having A No Hair Day!; Our Family Has Cancer, Too!* (written especially for children); *Inspiring Breakthrough Secrets to Live Your Dreams; Cancer Has Its Privileges: Stories of Hope & Laughter;* and *Your Guardian Angel's Gift.* Her two newest books are *Laugh 'Til It Heals: Notes from the World's Funniest Cancer Mailbox* and *The Clue Phone's Ringing . . . It's for You! Healing Humor for Women Divorcing.*

You, Inc.: The Art of Selling Yourself was released March 2007 by Warner Books and was named a "Notable Book of 2007" by the American Booksellers Association. Christine is also featured in the book *Masters of Sales.*

The year Christine faced a life-changing experience—she began her own company. Today The Cancer Club is the world's largest producer of humorous and helpful products for people with cancer. Christine's philosophies and strategies for becoming your industry's leader are proven theories that have propelled her and the companies she's worked with to the top of their fields. *Ideas, action, results . . .*

Christine is a contributing author to *Chicken Soup for the Survivor's Soul, Chicken Soup for the Golfer's Soul,* and *Chicken Soup for the Writer's Soul* and is featured in the books *The Courage to Laugh; The Triumph of the Human Spirit: Real Cancer Survivors, Real Battles, Real Victories; Gifts from the Train Station: Healing Yourself by Helping Others,* and *Masters of Sales.*

Featured in more than 3,000 media hits, including the *New York Times,* the *Wall Street Journal, Better Homes & Gardens, MORE* magazine, *American Health, Golf Digest, The Singapore Women's Weekly,* and the *Hindu* in India, she appeared on *CNN Live* in 1998 as "one of the world's leading authorities on the use of therapeutic humor."

Christine's inaugural event—*The Christine Clifford Celebrity Golf Tournament,* a benefit for breast cancer research—raised more than $100,000, making it the most successful first-year event in the history of the American Cancer Society. Her total contribution has been more than $1 million. Christine received the *Council of Excellence Award* for income development from the American Cancer Society.

In July 2002 Christine was awarded *The Order of the Delta Gamma Rose* from the sorority to confer special honor upon alumnae members who have made distinguished contributions to the nation or to the world through their individual efforts and talents and whose achievements have been given national recognition. It is the highest honor one can receive from the sorority and is awarded only every other year.

In July 2002 Christine also received her CSP (Certified Speaking Professional) designation from the National Speakers Association. The letters *CSP* following a speaker's name indicate a speaking professional with proven experience who brings a track record of experience and expertise. Less than 7 percent of the 5,000 speakers who belong to the International Federation for Professional Speakers hold this professional designation.

About the Author

Christine is a member of the National Speakers Association, the National Speakers Association—Minnesota Chapter, and the American Association for Applied and Therapeutic Humor. She is listed in *International Who's Who of Professionals, International Who's Who of Entrepreneurs,* and *International Who's Who of Authors and Writers.* She is also listed in *Contemporary Authors* and *2,000 Notable American Women.* She serves on the Board of Advisors for Minnesota Collegiate DECA.

In 2009, Christine helped launch a new multilevel marketing company, LifeVantage. She is also CEO/President of Divorcing Divas, LLC. Divorcing Divas, LLC, provides encouragement, inspiration, and empowerment to people going through the difficult process of divorce. Through support, education, resources, and hope, she shows divorcees that they can find life—and a good life—on the other side.

She has two grown sons, Tim and Brooks, and is grandmother to Siberian husky Skylar. She lives in Minneapolis, Minnesota.

Christine is available to speak to your organization about sales, marketing, or using humor to get through life's adversities. She provides sales and marketing consulting and strategic sales training.

For more information, please contact:

Christine Clifford Enterprises

P.O. Box 24747

Edina, MN 55424-0747

(612) 720-4974

Christine@christineclifford.com

www.christineclifford.com

www.cancerclub.com

www.DivorcingDivas.com

www.LifeVantage.com/LiveYoung

About the Author

Don't forget to ask!™
Don't forget to laugh!™
It's not the end . . . it's the beginning.

www.linkedin.com/in/christineclifford

www.facebook.com/#!/christine.k.clifford

www.facebook.com/#!/thecancerclub

www.facebook.com/#!/divorcingdivas

@c_clifford

@divorcingdivas

About Christine Clifford Enterprises

Spinning Ideas Into Action!

Christine Clifford has worked in a variety of industries with an extensive background in both packaged goods and service industries. But her specialty? Helping companies Spin Ideas Into Action.

Christine is available to provide keynote presentations or breakout sessions on sales and marketing for your organization or convention. Christine helps companies and individuals capture the essence of their story. Her services include:

- Vision and mission statements
- Company names and/or taglines
- Brand briefs
- Marketing brochures
- Custom press releases
- Client videos

Christine helps authors and speakers with the following services:

Authors

- Ghostwriting
- Editing
- Title and chapter selection
- Book proposals
- Testimonials
- Media attention
- Introduction to publishers and agents

Speakers

- Brand brief including target markets
- Custom marketing materials
- Demo videos
- Introduction to top 50 speakers' bureaus
- Coaching
- Media attention

Christine is available for consulting services on an hourly rate, per diem, or on a monthly retainer.

For more information about Christine Clifford Enterprises, call (952) 944-0639, e-mail us at Christine@christineclifford.com, or write:

Christine Clifford Enterprises

P.O. Box 24747

Edina, MN 55424-0747

www.christineclifford.com

About the Author